TURKEY, THE US AND IRAQ

Other titles in the series

Oil and Democracy in Iraq

British-Egyptian Relations from Suez to the Present Day

The Gulf Family: Kinship Policies and Modernity

SOAS MIDDLE EAST ISSUES

Turkey, the US and Iraq

William Hale

SAQI

in association with

LONDON
MIDDLE EAST
INSTITUTE
SOAS

ISBN (10): 0-86356-675-8
ISBN (13): 978-0-86356-675-2

© London Middle East Institute at SOAS, 2007

A full CIP record for this book is available from the British Library.
A full CIP record for this book is available from the Library of Congress.

Manufactured in the United Kingdom by CPI

SAQI

26 Westbourne Grove, London W2 5RH
825 Page Street, Suite 203, Berkeley, California 94710
Tabet Building, Mneimneh Street, Hamra, Beirut
www.saqibooks.com

in association with

The London Middle East Institute
School of Oriental and African Studies, Russell Square, London WC1H 0XG
www.lmei.soas.ac.uk

Contents

A Note on Spelling

Since 1928, Turkish has been written in a version of the Latin script, and this has been used for spelling Turkish personal and place names. In the modern Turkish alphabet, the letters are pronounced roughly as in English, with the following exceptions:

a – short 'a', as in French, or the English 'u' in 'hut'.

c – 'j', as in 'jam'.

ç – 'ch', as in 'church'.

ğ – normally silent: lengthens preceding vowel.

ı – as in the first and last 'a' in 'banana'.

i – as in 'bit': notice the upper case form İ.

ö – as in German, or the French 'eu' in 'leur'.

ş – 'sh', as in 'shut'.

ü – as in German, or the French 'u' in 'tu'.

Preface

The American-led invasion of Iraq in March 2003, and its long
and tortuous aftermath, has already produced a spate of literature,
and will doubtless go on producing more. This book does not seek
to duplicate it. Instead, it concentrates on the role and policies of
Turkey, as one of Iraq's most important neighbours, and America's
only formal ally in the region. To explain this, it starts the narrative
in the early 1920s, when the Iraqi state was first established, and
then examines the Turkish government's policies in the earlier Gulf
crisis of 1990–1. The story was full of contradictions and surprises.
In the First Gulf War, Turkey gave vital support to America, but in
2003 it strikingly failed to do so. On the second occasion, while
America sought to project itself as the champion of democracy
in the Middle East, Turkey, as the only Muslim country in the
region with an acceptably democratic form of government, refused
to support its strategy in Iraq. Effectively, the two parts of US
policy failed to cohere. For the Turks, also, the American strategy
presented some critical contradictions. On the one hand, Turkey
had a vital alliance with America, stretching back to the early days

of the cold war, and needed to sustain it. On the other hand, the Turkish government, since it was ultimately answerable to its own people, could not ignore their strong opposition to the invasion of Iraq. This produced serious tensions on the Turkish side, and unpredictable results. The outcome was ultimately less damaging than the likely alternatives, but this was as much the result of good luck as of good judgement on either side.

In writing this book, I have received vital help from a large number of friends and colleagues in Turkey and elsewhere. I am also deeply grateful to the School of Oriental and African Studies, at the University of London, which gave me generous research leave to allow me to complete it. To all of them, I must express my sincere thanks.

William Hale
Ankara, May 2006

ONE

Turkey and Iraq:
The Historical Background, 1918–80

Turkey's problems in its relations with Iraq, and their impact on its relationship with the leading world powers, go back to the territorial settlement in the Middle East which followed the First World War. Between 1534, when the armies of Sultan Suleyman the Magnificent captured Baghdad, and the defeat of Turkey at the end of the First World War in 1918, the territory of what is now Iraq was part of the Ottoman empire. It was administered as three provinces, based on Mosul in the north, Baghdad in the centre, and Basra in the south. Under the armistice of Mudros, signed by representatives of the defeated Ottoman government and Britain on 30 October 1918, the Turkish government accepted the British occupation of virtually all its former Arab provinces. Subsequently, the entente powers pushed forward an elaborate plan for the partition of the Ottoman Empire, including the territory of what is now the Republic of Turkey. This was formalized as the Treaty of Sèvres, which was signed by the government of the last Sultan Vahdettin (officially known as Mehmet VI) in August 1920.

The Sèvres treaty proposed, among other things, that a scheme for 'local autonomy' for the Kurds of south-eastern Anatolia should be worked out, possibly leading to an independent Kurdish state bordering what is now northern Iraq.[1] In the event, like the rest of the treaty, this proposal proved stillborn, since it was firmly rejected by the Turkish nationalist movement led by Mustafa Kemal, later Ataturk, who established a separate government in Ankara in April 1920. This de facto rebellion led to a war with the occupying entente forces, primarily Greece, ending in a decisive victory for the nationalist army in the autumn of 1922. Under the Treaty of Lausanne, signed in July 1923, the new Turkish state was recognized as independent and sovereign within virtually its present frontiers.[2] Following the abolition of the Ottoman Sultanate in November 1922, Turkey became a republic in October 1923, with Mustafa Kemal as its President and Ankara its capital. Meanwhile, in April 1920 the San Remo conference gave the British a League of Nations Mandate for their rule in Iraq. After an armed revolt by Arab and Kurdish tribes during June–October 1920, Britain established the Iraqi state in August 1921, under the nominal rule of its Hashemite ally, King Feisal I.[3]

Turkey, the Kurds and the Mosul Dispute: 1920–6

While the Lausanne treaty marked a decisive break with the Ottoman past, agreeing to the future shape of Iraq turned out to be the first serious diplomatic problem faced by the new Turkish republic. This dispute raised issues which are still important, and it thus needs some description. Like most of the subsequent story of relations between Iraq and Turkey, the most critical factor for both countries was that the majority of the population of northern Iraq and south-eastern Turkey was neither Turkish nor Arab, but Kurdish. (Northern Iraq also contains a minority of Turcomans, with ethnic links to the Turks, but this has not been a complicating factor in Turkish–Iraqi relations until very recently). In effect, both Turkey and Iraq acquired a Kurdish problem, in contiguous territories. In spite of the vague undertakings included in the Treaty of Sèvres, neither Turkey nor Britain accepted the idea of an independent Kurdish state. However, until 1926 Turkey persisted in its claim that the Mosul province should be part of its territory. This was strongly and successfully resisted by the British. Part of the Turkish case was legalistic, in the sense that the province had not been under British occupation at the time of the Mudros armistice, so that the Turks argued that they had never accepted its detachment from Turkey. More materially, at the start of their struggle against the entente, the Turkish nationalist leaders apparently expected that their future state would be a bi-national one, accepting both Turks and Kurds as distinct ethnic groups, and arguing that the Mosul province should thus be a legitimate part of it. This expectation was strengthened by the fact that the Kurds of Anatolia, as Muslims, generally supported the Turkish nationalists in their war against the Christian occupiers.

In January 1920 the last Ottoman Chamber of Deputies voted through the 'National Pact' (*Misak-i Milli*) which then became the founding charter of the national resistance movement. This accepted the loss of those 'portions of the Ottoman state which are populated exclusively by an Arab majority' and which were under occupation by the armies of the former entente at the time of the armistice of Mudros. By both definitions this apparently excluded Mosul, although this was not explicitly stated. Moreover, at no point did the pact refer to a specifically 'Turkish nation' or even a 'Turkish state'. Instead, it called for the independence and territorial integrity of those parts of the Ottoman Empire 'whether within or without the said armistice lines which are inhabited by an Ottoman Muslim [in effect, Turkish and Kurdish] majority'.[4] İsmet Pasha (later İsmet İnönü), the head of the Turkish delegation at Lausanne made this definition clearer when he claimed that there were no differences between the Turks and the Kurds, and that 'the Government of the Grand National Assembly [i.e. the Ankara government] is the Government of the Kurds just as much as the Government of the Turks'.[5] As a sign of this commitment, Mustafa Kemal and his colleagues considered ideas for the devolution of power to Kurdish-inhabited areas, to be included in the constitution of the new republic.[6]

The British and Turks also had their eyes on the rich oil resources of Kirkuk, although these did not begin production until 1927, and both sides denied that this was the main reason for their claim to Mosul.[7] On the British side, British companies had a dominant interest in the Turkish Petroleum Company, which had obtained an oil concession covering the Mosul province from the Ottoman government just before the First World War. In response, in April 1923 (before the conclusion of the Lausanne negotiations) the Ankara government granted a concession covering the oil rights to Mosul, as well as railway construction in Anatolia, to an American consortium headed by Admiral Colby M. Chester, Commander Arthur Chester and Colonel Clayton Kennedy (the 'Chester concession'). An important motive for this was apparently the hope that it might win American political support for the Turkish claim to Mosul.[8] Since the Chester consortium failed to deliver on its side of the deal, and the Harding administration in Washington was committed to isolationism, these hopes were frustrated, but it is clear that control over oil resources was already part of the dispute over northern Iraq, even at this early stage.

The Mosul question was the one major dispute between Turkey and the entente powers which was left unsettled when the Treaty of Lausanne was signed. Rather than let the peace conference drag on, the problem was left to separate negotiations between Britain and Turkey, with an agreement that the two sides would reach a settlement within nine months.[9] In fact, it was not until 1926, after lengthy arguments, that the Turkish government finally accepted the attachment of Mosul to Iraq. For the Turks, this represented a striking reversal of their initial position. There were a number of factors to explain this. Power politics, and the overall international situation, played an important role. As early as April 1922 Kemal had privately admitted that his battle-weary country could not go back to war, for the sake of Mosul (although he never made this public).[10] The British, however, may have been prepared to do so, so the Turks backed down.[11] Nor did world opinion, represented at the time by the League of Nations, favour the Turkish case. In the last analysis, Kemal decided it would be more important to establish good relations with the British than persist in the claim to Mosul.

Broader political changes in Turkey also contributed to this result. The principal bond between Turks and Kurds had been Islam, and the National Pact had thus referred to a religious, rather than secular ethnic identity as the basis of the national resistance.

However, in March 1924 Kemal's government took the first step in the foundation of a secular state, when it abolished the office of the Caliphate, representing the former Ottoman dynasty's claim to leadership of the Muslim world, and closed down all the separate religious educational institutions. This was reinforced in 1926, when the Islamic-based legal system was replaced by secular legal codes largely imported from Italy, Switzerland and France, although a reference to Islam as the religion of the state was not removed from the constitution until 1928. As Caroline Finkel succinctly puts it, 'the unravelling of the empire dissolved the bonds that had united Turks and Kurds – the sultanate, Islamic law and the Caliphate'.[12] Since the new state's legitimacy was to be based on 'Turkishness', rather than attachment to Islam, its claim to Mosul, with its Kurdish and Arab population, was fatally weakened. When the first full constitution of the Turkish republic was adopted in April 1924, the earlier proposals for regional devolution were dropped, and the constitution provided for a highly centralized unitary state. After 1925, even the existence of the Kurdish minority in Turkey was denied. Although only the most extreme Turkish nationalists still advance this view, there was much pseudo-scholarly argument designed to 'prove' that the Kurds were really 'mountain Turks', who had somehow adopted the Kurdish language.[13] Any expression of a separate Kurdish identity was made illegal and people were even fined for using Kurdish in public.

This change of heart was strengthened by practical experience in March 1925, when a rebellion broke out in south-eastern Anatolia led by a Kurdish tribal and religious leader, Sheikh Sayid of Palu.[14] The rebellion appears to have had a number of motives. Kurdish separatism almost certainly played a role, but Sheikh Sayid also tried to appeal to those who opposed the abolition of the Caliphate, whatever their ethnicity, and was opposed by some Kurdish tribes, who refused to join the revolt, as well as the Turkish army. There are also persistent Turkish suspicions that the British had a hand in the rebellion, although it was rapidly crushed in draconian fashion. Whatever the truth, it was clear that Kurdish rebellions were a potential threat to the Turkish state, and that Mosul, with its predominantly Kurdish population, would be more of a political liability than an asset to Turkey. This consideration still affects Turkish attitudes, even if these are sometimes ambivalent.

In spite of these considerations, Kemal's government was slow to abandon its claim. Following the failure of direct negotiations between Turkey and Britain, the British government referred the Mosul question to the League of Nations in August 1924. In July 1925 a Commission of Inquiry established by the League reported that the province should be awarded to Iraq, but Turkey (which was not a member of the League at the time) rejected this. The Permanent Court of International Justice then decided that a decision by the Council of the League would be binding on both parties, leaving the Council to issue a unanimous decision in favour of Iraq in December 1925. After much reluctance, and under possible threat of war by Britain, the Turkish government accepted this under a treaty signed with the British in June 1926, and a tripartite Anglo-Turkish-Iraqi treaty of the following month.[15] As part of the deal, Turkey was to receive 10 per cent of the oil royalties paid to the Iraqi government from production in Mosul for twenty-five years: these payments began in 1931 and continued until 1955.[16]

Turkey and Iraq: Changing Fortunes, 1926–80

After 1926, Turkey generally turned its back on the Middle East: its main security concerns lay in Europe, especially with the rise of Mussolini as a potential aggressor in the Mediterranean and the Balkans during the early 1930s. Culturally, the historical link with the Arab and Muslim worlds was ignored – for instance, in school textbooks – as Turkey sought to make itself a respected member of the Western comity of nations. In the Middle East, stability and security on its southern and eastern frontiers was all it required. As part of this process, the 1926 treaty with the British gradually paved the way for the strengthening of its relations with Iraq, which was recognized as an independent state and a member of the League of Nations in 1932 (Turkey joined the League in the same year). In July 1937 Turkey joined Iraq, Iran and Afghanistan in concluding the Saadabad Pact, named after the Shah's palace near Tehran where it was signed. Although the pact is sometimes presented as an anti-Soviet alliance, it had no provisions for mutual assistance or military obligations, but merely committed the signatories to respect their mutual frontiers, not to interfere in one another's internal affairs or commit aggression against one another's territory, and to consult on matters of common interest. The first two provisions were almost certainly the most important ones for the four governments. On the Iraqi side, for instance, it was important to ensure that Iran respected the Iran–Iraq frontier treaty of the same month, giving Iraq sovereignty over all but a small part of the Shatt al-Arab river which formed the southern part of its frontier with Iran. For Turkey the pact served to ensure that, for instance, Kurdish rebels in Turkey did not operate through Iranian territory, as they had in an insurrection in the region of Mount

Ararat in 1929–30. The confirmation of the existing Turkish–Iraqi border was also another signal that Turkey had formally abandoned its claim to Mosul.[17]

During the Second World War, Turkey was a de facto neutral, although officially allied with Britain and France by a treaty signed in October 1939. However, it became involved in events in the Middle East, thanks to the crisis in Iraq in 1941. Following a *coup d'état* in Baghdad on 1 April, the nationalist Iraqi politician Rashid Ali al-Kailani became Prime Minister. The Regent of Iraq, Abd al-Ilah and the former Prime Minister Nuri al-Sa'id, who both favoured the British, took refuge in Transjordan. The British refused to recognize Rashid Ali's government. In response, Rashid Ali tried to restrict the British ability to reinforce their troops in Iraq, and Iraqi forces surrounded the British air base at Habbaniyyah, west of Baghdad. Late in the day, as the British were preparing to re-occupy Iraq, Rashid Ali appealed to Germany for support, via the German embassy in Ankara. Hitler responded on 3 May, by agreeing to send some German warplanes and arms to Iraq, but at this stage he was heavily engaged in the Balkans and in preparations for his invasion of the USSR, which began in the following month. The quickest way for Germany to send arms to Iraq was to draw on French stocks in Syria, which at this time was controlled by the Vichy collaborationist government. However, the only railway from Syria to Iraq ran across Turkish territory, so the operation depended on the compliance of the Turkish authorities. According to one account, the Turkish government sought to exploit the situation by sending its own forces to Iraq, hoping to achieve this by collaborating with either Germany or Britain.[18] However, in practice, the furthest it was prepared to go was to allow four train-loads of arms to reach Iraq from Syria in the second half of May.

In the event, these and the thirty or so German warplanes sent to Iraq had virtually no effect on the outcome.[19] While the Turkish government made unsuccessful attempts to mediate between Rashid Ali and the British, it also resisted demands from Germany to be allowed to send unlimited quantities of arms and a defined number of German troops to Iraq across Turkey. In the meantime, the British and their allies had re-entered Iraq in force and deposed Rashid Ali by 30 May 1941, going on to overthrow the pro-Vichy forces in Syria by mid-July.[20] This saved Turkey from what could have been a very dangerous situation: had the British not acted when they did, then it could have been surrounded by the existing German forces in Greece and Bulgaria to the west, and German or pro-German forces in Syria and Iraq to the south. Hitler's invasion of the USSR in June 1941 was also a stroke of luck for Turkey, since it meant that he would not have sufficient forces available for a campaign in the Middle East unless and until the Soviet Union were defeated.

During the post-war period, Turkey's relations with Iraq were largely determined as a by-product of the cold war, and internal political divisions in Baghdad. After 1945 Turkey's main security concern was that it might be attacked by the Soviet Union, and to counter this it sought firm security guarantees from the Western powers. When the North Atlantic Treaty was signed in April 1949 Turkey and Greece were excluded from the Western Alliance, and it was not until March 1951 that the US government decided that they should be admitted to NATO. Turkey's bid for full membership of the alliance was held up by a British attempt to make this conditional upon Turkish membership of a proposed Middle East Command, under which Turkish troops would be placed under British command in the event of war. In effect, the British sought to use Turkey to prop up their declining power in the region. The Turkish and US governments successfully resisted this, so that Greece and Turkey were eventually admitted to full membership of NATO in February 1952 without this condition. However, as a concession to the British, the government of Prime Minister Adnan Menderes in Ankara agreed that it would take on an undefined defence role in the Middle East.[21] In 1955, this took shape as the Baghdad Pact, embracing Turkey, Iraq, Iran, Pakistan and Britain. The United States never became a formal signatory of the pact, but throughout it was its most powerful sponsor, seeing the pact as part of a chain of alliances to contain the Soviet Union.

From the start, the Baghdad Pact suffered from serious weaknesses. Unlike NATO, it had no centralized military command structure, and committed its members to no more than a pledge of mutual assistance in the event of external aggression (by implication, from the USSR). It had originally been hoped that other leading Arab states, including Egypt, Jordan and Syria, would join the pact, but they vociferously rejected it, leaving Iraq as the pact's only Arab member. In its original shape, the survival of the pact depended on that of the Iraqi premier Nuri al-Sa'id, who supported it since it gave Iraq control over the British air-bases in Iraq while maintaining military cooperation with Britain and preserving Iraqi independence in the face of rising pan-Arabist nationalism. However, precisely for these reasons, it was opposed by a large body of Iraqi opinion, notably in the army, which overthrew both Nuri and the monarchy itself in a violent *coup d'état* on 14 July 1958. Nuri,

King Feisal II, Crown Prince Abd al-Ilah and their relatives were lynched by the mob. The leader of the coup, Brigadier Abd al-Karim Qasim became Prime Minister, Minister of Defence, and Commander-in-Chief of the new Iraqi republic. From this point on, Iraq's participation in the pact effectively ceased. The headquarters of the alliance was moved from Baghdad to Ankara in October 1958, although Iraq did not formally withdraw its membership until December 1959.[22] Meanwhile, the pact changed its title to the Central Treaty Organization (CENTO) in August 1959, and continued in that form until the Iranian revolution of 1979.

After the overthrow of Adnan Menderes by another *coup d'état*, this time in Ankara, on 27 May 1960, the Baghdad Pact, and Turkey's role in it, came in for sharp criticism in Turkey, mainly on the grounds that it had subordinated Turkey's national interests (of maintaining good relations with the Arab countries, so far as possible) to those of the United States.[23] In fairness to Menderes, it has to be said that this was a classic case of being wise after the event. At the time the pact was signed, it had general support in Ankara, including that of the opposition Republican People's Party (CHP) led by İsmet İnönü. Menderes promoted the pact not just because this would please the United States, but because, like the then US Secretary of State John Foster Dulles, he genuinely believed in the threat of communist subversion and takeover in the Middle East, and thought that the pact would be the best way of defeating it. He and the then Turkish president, Celal Bayar, played an active role in trying to persuade Syria, Lebanon and Jordan to join the pact, and failed to anticipate the hostility it would face in most of the Arab world.[24] At the bilateral level, the connection with Iraq was fortified by personal relationships, and not just political convenience.

Menderes regarded Nuri al-Sa'id as a personal friend, while the young King Feisal II was a fairly frequent visitor to Istanbul, and was engaged to Princess Fazileh, a descendant of the formal royal Ottoman dynasty. The violent overthrow of the old regime in Baghdad set off shock waves in Turkey, since it took place on the day the King had been due to arrive in Istanbul in preparation for a forthcoming meeting of the pact members. In the aftermath of the coup, Menderes even proposed a military intervention in Iraq to restore a pro-Western regime, but this scheme was dropped under US pressure and objections from the Turkish military chiefs, who cited the lack of roads in the border region.[25]

What is perhaps surprising is that, following the overthrow of the Iraqi monarchy, Turkish–Iraqi relations were restored quite rapidly. After 1958, the Turkish government was realistic enough to recognize that the Baghdad Pact, in its original shape, was dead and buried, and that Turkey needed to establish working relations with the new Iraqi regime. Accordingly a Turkish delegation attended the celebrations in Baghdad, held to mark the first anniversary of the coup in July 1959. A reconciliation with the Iraqi revolutionaries was also made easier because Qasim refused to join the then United Arab Republic of Egypt and Syria. In Middle Eastern politics, he could be expected to act as a counterweight to the Egyptian President Gemal Abd al-Nasser.[26] Once it was clear that Iraq would continue as an independent state, Turkey was satisfied since, by itself, it was not strong enough to threaten Turkey's security, while Turkey could not take on the political and military risks of an attack on Iraq. More widely, the collapse of the Baghdad Pact persuaded Turkish policy-makers that they would do best to detach their policies in the Middle East from their alliance with the Western powers, dealing with each of the regional states on an individual and pragmatic basis. Nor should Turkey side with any of them in disputes with their neighbours. In this way, Turkish–Iraqi relations attained a stable plateau, which survived frequent changes of government in both countries. In Turkey, the Kurdish-inhabited south-east was comparatively peaceful until the late 1970s, when fighting re-erupted between the Turkish security forces and a number of rival Kurdish militant organizations, but this could be seen as part of a much wider problem of terrorism by leftist and ultra-rightist gangs which led to a general breakdown of law and order, ended by a takeover by the military on 12 September 1980. In Iraq there were Kurdish rebellions led by Mustafa Barzani's Kurdistan Democratic Party in 1961–3, 1964–6, 1968–9, and 1974–5. On each occasion, Turkey was happy to stand aside, since events in Iraq at the time did not appear to have had any significant effect on the Turkish Kurds.

The political relationship between the two countries was also strengthened by growing economic links, most notably the opening of an oil pipeline between Kirkuk and the port of Yumurtalık, near Adana, on Turkey's Mediterranean coast, in 1977. The sharp rise in oil prices in 1973–4, as well as Turkey's growing oil consumption, increased the share of the oil-producing countries, such as Iraq, in its total foreign trade: after some delay, this led to an impressive rise in Turkey's exports to the region.[27] All this increased Turkey's incentive to maintain good relations with Iraq, in spite of its unstable and frequently violent domestic politics.

Turkey and Iraq: Assumptions and Ground-rules

Experiences on both sides since the early 1920s had shown that this reasonably satisfactory situation in Turkish–Iraqi relations was – and still is – dependent on certain basic conditions. One is the continuation of a rough balance of power between the two countries, so that neither is in a position to seriously threaten the security of the other. More broadly, this may be seen as a four-state power balance, including Syria and Iran as well as Turkey and Iraq. By most conventional yardsticks, Turkey is the most powerful of the four states, since it has a big population, large and well-equipped armed forces (buttressed by the NATO alliance) and a more diversified economy. However, in line with the cultural reorientation established by Ataturk, it has tended to see itself as a 'Western' rather than Middle Eastern power, and has not normally aimed to be a regional hegemon – indeed, it is most unlikely that it could succeed in such a project even if it tried to. This balance of power naturally depends on the survival of both Turkey and Iraq as independent states, which are not taken over by or merged with other regional actors, and are able to maintain state power within their frontiers. In the Turkish case, this factor has never been seriously problematic, since Turkey has its own distinct political and cultural identity, so is most unlikely to merge with other states. At the same time, it is strong enough to prevent a takeover by any of its neighbours, and to maintain control over its own territory. In the Iraqi case, the first condition has not always been secure. As Arabs, in the 1950s and 1960s, many Iraqis responded to the call for Arab unity. In 1958 there seemed to be a real risk of a tripartite merger between Iraq, Syria and Egypt, to Turkey's disadvantage (the contemporary entente between the last two and the USSR appeared to exacerbate the danger). Fortunately for Turkey, this was never achieved. Arab unity, as a state-building project, has dropped off the Middle Eastern political agenda since 1967. Instead, Iraq has generally acted as a rival to Syria, with which Turkey has in turn had serious territorial and other disputes.

A second condition is obviously that each country respects the frontier established in 1926 and does not have territorial ambitions against the other. On the Iraqi side, this has never been in serious doubt, since Iraq gained territorially by the 1926 settlement and has no interest in altering it. In Turkey, ambitious or ultra-nationalist politicians have occasionally and tentatively tried to resurrect the claim to Mosul, which was only reluctantly accepted in 1926 (see pp. 45–6, 97). However, no Turkish government has ever denounced the 1926 frontier – indeed it has twice been confirmed since then, by the Saadabad and Baghdad Pacts – and reviving the claim to Mosul has never been part of the accepted policy of any Turkish government. Since 1923, Turkey has generally acted as a pro-status quo power, putting emphasis on the need to respect international treaties unless they are altered by mutual agreement, especially, in its relations with Greece and the Republic of Cyprus.[28] It cannot afford to abandon this principle for the sake of Mosul, where in any case its claim would in practice be impossible to sustain, either politically or militarily.

Essentially, the Ankara–Baghdad axis has also depended on joint opposition to Kurdish national aspirations. Since the 1920s both states have adhered to this principle. Neither has followed the tactics of Iran, which gave full backing to the Kurdish rebellion in Iraq in 1974–5, for fear that this would backfire by encouraging Kurdish separatism in their own territory. As a result, the Turkish government had no contacts with the Iraqi Kurds, and virtually ignored their existence, until 1991. However, suppressing Kurdish nationalism has not been easy, especially if state power in the Kurdish regions of either country breaks down on a long-term basis, or Kurdish nationalists receive powerful and lasting outside support. Until the 1990s this was generally avoided. Since 1991, however, the outcome of the Gulf war of that year and the establishment of the United States as a leading military actor in the region, has radically altered the picture, especially in Iraq. In this way Turkish–Iraqi relations have become deeply affected by US policies. The binary Ankara–Baghdad relationship has in effect become a triangular one, with Washington as the third corner, hugely complicating the tasks of policy-making. Similarly, domestic developments in Iraq have become a major focus of concern for Turkey.

Notes

1. For the text of the treaty, see J. C. Hurewitz, ed., *Diplomacy in the Near and Middle East: A Diplomatic Record, 1914–1956*, vol. 2, Princeton NJ: Van Nostrand, 1956, pp. 81–9.
2. Two exceptions were, first, the province of Mosul, whose status was left undecided at Lausanne, and the province of İskenderun (Alexandretta) which was annexed by Turkey from French-ruled Syria in 1939.
3. See Charles Tripp, *A History of Iraq*, Cambridge: Cambridge University Press, 2000, pp. 41–9.
4. For the full text, see Hurewitz, ed., *Diplomacy*, vol. 2, pp. 74–5. For an overall account of these events, and of Turkish foreign policy in general during the inter-war years, see William Hale, *Turkish Foreign Policy, 1774–2000*, 2nd edn, London and Portland OR: Frank Cass, 2002, ch. 2.
5. Quoted, David McDowall, *A Modern History of the Kurds*, London: I. B. Tauris, 1996, p. 190.
6. See Andrew Mango, 'Ataturk and the Kurds', *Middle Eastern Studies*, vol. 35, no. 4, 1999, pp. 13–16.
7. Peter J. Beck, "'A Tedious and Perilous Controversy": Britain and the

Settlement of the Mosul Dispute', *Middle Eastern Studies*, vol. 17, no. 2, 1981, p. 159. Beck points out, however, that 'even without oil, the British government would have been reluctant to make concessions on Mosul', since its main motive was strategic.

8. Selim İlkin, 'The Chester Railway Project', in Türkiye İş Bankası, *International Symposium on Ataturk (17–22 May 1981)*, Ankara: Türkiye İş Bankası Kültür Yayınları, 1984, pp. 769–817.

9. Beck, 'Mosul Dispute', pp. 256–61.

10. Doğu Perincek, ed., *Mustafa Kemal Eskişehir İzmit Konuşmaları*, Istanbul: Kaynak, 1993, pp. 94–7.

11. In 1925, at a late stage of the dispute, the British prepared plans to block the Dardanelles so as to force Turkey to climb down over Mosul. Whether they were prepared to go through with this may be doubtful, but the Turks evidently decided that the risk was not worth taking: see Beck, 'Mosul Dispute', pp. 268–9.

12. Caroline Finkel, *Osman's Dream: The Story of the Ottoman Empire, 1300– 1923*, London: John Murray, 2005, p. 549.

13. One should perhaps say 'languages', since the Turkish Kurds speak both Zaza and Kirmanji. See Paul B. Henze, 'Turkey: Toward the Twenty-First Century', in Graham E. Fuller and Ian O. Lesser, eds, *Turkey's New Geopolitics: From the Balkans to Western China*, Boulder, CO: Westview, 1993, p. 22.

14. For a succinct account, see McDowall, *Modern History*, pp. 194–8.

15. See ibid. pp. 143–6: Beck, 'Mosul Dispute', pp. 261–73: Stephen F. Evans, *The Slow Rapprochement: Britain and Turkey in the Age of Kemal Ataturk*, Walkington: Eothen Press, 1982, pp. 80–97.

16. Nevin Coşar and Sevtap Demirci, 'The Mosul Question and the Turkish Republic: Before and After the Frontier Treaty, 1926', *Middle Eastern Studies*, vol. 42, no. 1, 2006, pp. 128–31.

17. McDowall, *Modern History*, pp. 204–6; Tripp, *History of Iraq*, pp. 90–1; A Suat Bilge, et al., *Olaylarla Türk Dış Politikası (1919–1965)*, Ankara University, Political Science Faculty, 1969, pp. 114–7; Aptülhat Akşin, *Atatürk'ün Dış Politika İlkeleri ve Diplomasisi*, Ankara: Türk Tarih Kurumu, 1991, pp. 198–9.

18. According to a private letter from Sir Hughe Knatchbull-Hugessen, the British ambassador in Ankara, to Sir Orme Sargent, Deputy Under Secretary of State in the Foreign Office, which was written almost a year later in April 1942. See Frank G. Weber, *The Evasive Neutral: Germany, Britain and the Quest for a Turkish Alliance in the Second World War*, Columbia MO and London: University of Missouri Press, 1979, pp. 89–90.

19. Lukasz Hirszowicz, *The Third Reich and the Arab East*, London: Routledge & Kegan Paul, 1966, pp. 159–64. For a slightly different account, see Selim Deringil, *Turkish Foreign Policy during the Second World War: An 'Active' Neutrality*, Cambridge: Cambridge University Press, 1989, pp. 124–5.

20. Hirszowicz, *Third Reich*, pp. 181–4; Tripp, *History of Iraq*, pp. 103–5; Y. Olmert, 'Britain, Turkey and the Levant Question during the Second World War', *Middle Eastern Studies*, vol. 23, no. 4, 1987, pp. 444–7.

21. John C. Campbell, *Defense of the Middle East: Problems of American Policy*, New York: Praeger, 1960, pp. 40–8; Ekavi Athanassopoulou, *Turkey–Anglo-American Security Interests, 1945–1952: The First Enlargement of NATO*, London: Cass, 1999, pp. 218–20 and 227–8; George C. McGhee, *The US–Turkish–NATO Middle East Connection*, London: Macmillan, 1990, pp. 87–8; Bilge, et al., *Olaylarla*, pp. 247–52.

22. Ara Sanjian, 'The Formulation of the Baghdad Pact', *Middle Eastern Studies*, vol. 33, no. 2, 1997, pp. 237, 242–5 and 259; Aysegul Sever, 'The Compliant Ally? Turkey and the West in the Middle East, 1954–58', *Middle Eastern Studies*, vol. 34, no. 2, 1998, p. 75; Campbell, *Defense*, pp. 49–54; Bilge, et al., *Olaylarla*, pp. 237–88; Tripp, *History of Iraq*, pp. 140–7.

23. Kemal H. Karpat, 'Turkish and Arab–Israeli Relations', in Karpat et al., *Turkey's Foreign Policy in Transition*, Leiden: Brill, 1975, pp. 122–5.

24. Mustafa Albayrak, *Türk Siyasi Tarihinde Demokrat Parti*, Ankara: Phoenix, 2004, pp. 474–6.

25. Ibid. pp. 478–9; George S. Harris, *Troubled Alliance: Turkish–American Problems in Historical Perpective, 1945–1971*, Washington DC: American Enterprise Institute for Public Policy Research and Hoover Institution, 1972, pp. 65–6; Richard D. Robinson, *The First Turkish Republic*, Cambridge MA: Harvard University Press, 1963, p. 187. On similar contemporaneous proposals by British and US military planners, see Stephen Blackwell, 'A Desert Squall: Anglo-American Planning for Military Intervention in Iraq, July 1958–August 1959', *Middle Eastern Studies*, vol. 35, no. 3, 1999, pp. 3–4.

26. Ferenc A. Vali, *Bridge Across the Bosporus: The Foreign Policy of Turkey*, Baltimore MD and London; Johns Hopkins University Press, 1971, p. 301.

27. See Philip Robins, *Turkey and the Middle East*, London: Pinter, for Royal Institute of International Affairs, 1991, pp. 100–7.

28. The two treaties concerned in these cases are the Treaty of Lausanne of 1923, and the Treaty of Guarantee regarding Cyprus, between Britain, Greece, Cyprus and Turkey, of 1960.

TWO

Turkey, Iraq and the Kuwait Crisis, 1980–93

During the late 1970s Turkish politics were drifting into chaos as a series of coalition or minority governments, led alternately by Bülent Ecevit, of the centre-left Republican People's Party or by Süleyman Demirel of the centre-right Justice Party, failed to suppress a rising tide of violence by political desperadoes of the extreme left and right, or to cope with a collapsing economy. The result was another *coup d'état* on 12 September 1980, installing a military regime under General Kenan Evren which lasted until November 1983. In that month, general elections were held, resulting in the victory of the Motherland Party, led by Turgut Özal. Özal was to become the dominant personality in Turkish politics for the next decade, serving as Prime Minister between 1983 and 1989, when he succeeded Kenan Evren as President of the Republic, until his untimely death from a heart attack in

April 1993. Meanwhile, in Iraq, Saddam Hussein had gradually taken over power from his kinsman, President Ahmad Hasan al-Bakr, becoming President of Iraq in July 1979. In September 1980 he launched a war against Iran which continued until July 1988, causing huge costs and casualties, with no ultimate advantage to either side.

In Turkey, Özal's main achievements were economic. As Minister of State with special responsibility for the economy in the last pre-coup government, between January and September 1980, and then as Deputy Prime Minister under the military until July 1982, he had begun a programme of radical reforms, aimed at ending Turkey's periodic chronic inflation and balance of payments crises by opening up the economy to market mechanisms and world conditions. He continued this vigorously after 1983, by reducing government controls, freeing interest and foreign exchange rates, and liberalizing foreign trade. Until the late 1980s, this programme brought impressive results, including restored economic growth, a sharp increase in exports and increased investor confidence. By the end of the decade, however, it was running out of steam, with continued inflation and widespread allegations of government corruption, resulting in the Motherland Party's loss of its parliamentary majority in the general elections of October 1991.

In foreign policy, Turgut Özal could be less predictable, although not initially adventurous. As one of his closest colleagues, Güneş Taner, remarked after his death:

> Özal was like a sponge. He would seize on whatever was novel in what you were saying, then sell it on as if it were his own. He showed us vision, gathered light and focused it like a spotlight.[1]

31

Until the late 1970s, he had Islamist political sympathies, having unsuccessfully run as a candidate in the 1977 general elections for the pro-Islamist National Salvation Party, headed by Necmettin Erbakan, of which his brother Korkut Özal was deputy leader.[2] Although he continued to be an observant Muslim throughout his life, once in office, Turgut Özal effectively abandoned Islamism as a political credo, replacing it with liberal conservatism. In essence he believed that Islam as a religion could be combined with modernity, within a liberal perspective.[3] In foreign policy, he was a firm advocate of Turkey's association with the West, and its alliance with the United States. In the Middle East, as in other regions, he advocated the adoption of an economic pact providing for free trade and economic cooperation. This approach may have been unrealistically optimistic, but it seems to have been firmly held nonetheless, and was combined with the belief that, in Turkey's case, there were no fundamental contradictions between Turkey's interests and those of the West – the United States in particular. In this way, Özal was willing to fit into US strategies which saw Turkey as a bulwark against militant Islamism, headed by post-revolutionary Iran.[4]

Turkey and Iraq, 1983–90

During the 1980s Özal's government did not seek to break with the main lines of policy towards Iraq which had been established after the collapse of the Baghdad Pact – that is to say that Turkey should maintain good relations with the Iraqi government, whatever its political colouring, and not take sides in disputes between it and other Middle Eastern states. An example of this was Turkish policy during the Iran–Iraq war, which applied strict neutrality, and sought to exploit the increased dependence on Turkey of both the belligerents, especially in the economic sphere. Thanks to the war, Iran as well as Iraq became significantly dependent on Turkish goodwill for trade and transit traffic, due to the difficulty of maintaining normal traffic through the Gulf.[5] Turkey won important economic benefits, as its exports to the two countries increased from US$220 million in 1980 to US$2,040 million in 1985, at which point they accounted for over a quarter of its total exports. In the case of trade with Iraq, Turkey's imports, which consisted almost entirely of crude oil, remained steady at around US$1.1 billion per year, while its exports, which consisted mainly of foodstuffs, other consumer goods and construction materials, increased from US$135 million in 1980 to US$961 million in 1985. These figures fell back in 1986–8, but mainly because Iraq, like Iran, began to run short of funds, rather than any policy shift by Turkey: in fact at the end of the war Iraq had substantial unpaid commercial debts to Turkey, as to other countries.[6] For Iraq, the Kirkuk–Yumurtalık oil pipeline (see p. 24) was a vital connection, given the closure of its normal export routes through the Gulf, and its capacity was expanded from one million barrels to 1.5 million barrels per day in 1987. Strategically, the Turks were also lucky that neither of the belligerents were able to win an outright victory, which might have left them free to adopt more aggressive policies towards Turkey.

Meanwhile, the only potentially serious dispute between Turkey and Iraq concerned the waters of the river Euphrates, which flows from Turkish territory into Syria and then Iraq, and on which both the downstream countries are dependent for irrigation. This did not reach a head until 1990, just before the Gulf crisis of that year, when the Turkish authorities cut back the cross-border flow in order to fill the reservoir behind the massive Ataturk dam, recently completed in the Turkish section of the river. While Turkey's water dispute was mainly with Syria, rather than Iraq, the Iraqi government was also involved, and sharply critical of Turkish policies. In May 1990, Yıldırım Akbulut, who had become Prime Minister and leader of the Motherland Party after Özal's election as President in the previous year, paid a visit to Baghdad in a fruitless attempt to settle the issue. Shortly afterwards, Iraq was effectively lifted out of the dispute by its occupation of Kuwait, and consequent international isolation.[7]

On the other hand, as in previous years, common opposition to Kurdish separatism was also a basic principle in both Turkish and Iraqi policies. This was particularly important for Turkey, since militant Kurdish resistance to Ankara re-emerged in the 1980s, following its temporary suppression by the military regime. In 1984 the Kurdistan Worker's Party (*Partiya Karkeren Kurdistan*, or PKK), founded and led by Abdullah Öcalan and supported by Syria as well as sympathizers in Europe and in Turkey itself, launched a campaign of violence, with terrorist attacks on civilian targets (mainly its fellow-Kurds) as well as the Turkish army and police. Under Özal, the Turkish army responded by mounting a counter-insurgency campaign. In the Kurdish-inhabited provinces of south-eastern Anatolia, martial law, originally imposed by the military government of 1980–3, was replaced in 1987 by an 'Emergency Situation' regime, in which the police and army were given exceptional powers, and civil rights severely restricted. In Iraq, the war with Iran also allowed the Iraqi Kurds to re-start their rebellion against Baghdad, as the Kurdistan Democratic

Party (KDP), now led by Mustafa Barzani's son Massoud Barzani, cooperated with the Iranians in capturing border areas in 1983.[8] Until 1985 the rebellion was weakened by the fact that Barzani's main Kurdish rival, Jelal Talabani, leader of the Patriotic Union of Kurdistan (PUK), refused to join it, and continued negotiations with Saddam's government. However, by mid-1985, Talabani had abandoned this tactic, and joined forces with Barzani, strengthening the revolt.[9] Turkey and Iraq were, for the first time, faced with simultaneous Kurdish insurgency.

For Turkey, an important effect of the renewed Kurdish revolt in Iraq was that it gave the PKK a haven in parts of northern Iraq, over which Saddam's forces had lost control. To counter this, in February 1983, the military-controlled administration had concluded a 'Frontier Security and Cooperation Agreement' with Iraq under which the two governments were entitled to carry out 'hot pursuit' operations against armed groups in each other's territory. In 1984 this was extended by a Security Protocol which defined hot pursuit operations as those conducted up to 5 kilometres within the territory of either signatory. The Turkish forces made use of these arrangements in 1983, 1986 and 1987. Evidently, Saddam Hussein was prepared to accept these incursions, since they weakened his own Kurdish opponents. In the course of these operations, Turkish forces also attacked camps of the KDP and PUK. Politically, this had the opposite effect to that intended, since it brought about an anti-Turkish alliance between the PKK and the Iraqi Kurdish leadership. The alliance lasted until 1987, when Barzani broke it off, inducing the PKK to opt for a unilateral entente with the PUK.[10]

This heralded the beginnings of a shift in Turkish policies at the very end of the Iran–Iraq war. In March 1988, Iranian forces captured the town of Halabjah, in Iraqi Kurdistan, raising fears on the Turkish side that they might go on to take Kirkuk. However, in the following July, Iraqi forces recaptured Halabjah, subjecting the town to a horrific poison gas attack in which about 5,000 innocent civilians died. Iran then accepted a UN brokered cease-fire, and the war was formally at an end. Saddam Hussein used this opportunity to wreak his revenge on the Kurds. In a savage campaign codenamed *al-Anfal* ('the spoils'), 800 Kurdish villages were destroyed, about 250,000 people were forcibly resettled in the south and centre of Iraq, and the Turkish–Iraqi border region was left uninhabited. In August the Iraqi forces again used chemical weapons against remaining Kurdish militia who were fleeing to the Turkish frontier.

Initially, the Turkish authorities refused to allow the refugees into their country but then, realizing they faced a humanitarian catastrophe, they relented. The Iraqi government claimed the right to pursue them into Turkish territory, under the 1983 and 1984 agreements, but this was refused by Turkey, which replied that they would be disarmed and prevented from carrying out any further operations against Iraq. In response, Iraq unilaterally abrogated the 'hot pursuit' agreements. By September 1988 some 63,000 Kurdish refugees had been settled 'temporarily' in Turkey, in twelve refugee camps in south-east Anatolia. Officially, they were not given the status of refugees, and their treatment by the Turkish authorities was a source of frequent criticism by Western humanitarian organizations.[11] However, the incident had forced the Turkish government into the realization that the Iraqi Kurds would not inevitably be enemies. It also seems to have produced an important effect on Özal's attitude towards Saddam Hussein. Until 1988, like other Turkish policy makers, he had apparently been prepared to overlook the fact that Saddam was a ruthless tyrant, so long as he did not damage Turkey's national interests. According to a later statement by Güneş Taner, the events of 1988 upset him seriously. Özal came to the conclusion that the Iraqi dictator was a despot lacking in normal human values, and that he could use his horrific weapons against anyone, including Turkey. He would eventually have to be 'purged'.[12] These observations, plus the emergence of the Euphrates dispute as an issue between Iraq and Turkey in 1990, suggest that, even before the Iraqi invasion of Kuwait, Turkish–Iraqi relations were already heading for conflict, after the years of implicit, if not explicit, cooperation.

Turkey and the Gulf Crisis, August 1990 to January 1991

The crisis caused by Iraq's invasion of Kuwait on 2 August 1990 was a turning point in Turkey's policy towards the Middle East. The reasons are not hard to identify. In the first place, it has to be remembered that the invasion had not been generally expected (although, as explained below, Özal himself apparently had some expectations of the kind several months previously). Even if they had thought previously that Iraqi aggression against Kuwait might occur, none of the regional or global actors appear to have decided in advance what their reactions would be, or how they would coordinate their approaches. Policies had to be formulated rapidly and on the hoof, with many previous assumptions hastily abandoned.

As is usual in such circumstances, crisis management in unexpected situations put a premium on instant decisions. Turkey's traditional foreign policy making mechanism, which assumed the forging of a consensus between the President, the government, the foreign ministry and the armed forces commanders, was poorly adapted to coping with this situation, especially if there were disagreements between them. As head of state, and a more experienced politician than any other member of the government, Özal emerged as a powerful foreign policy-maker, whose frequent contacts with other world leaders appeared to place him in the driving seat. Since Turkey is a parliamentary rather than presidential republic, this threatened to reverse the normal and constitutionally legitimate situation in which the Prime Minister and the cabinet, not the President, are the final decision makers. Telephone diplomacy put Özal in constant contact with President George Bush and other world leaders, who evidently expected him to make decisions on behalf of Turkey. However, his policies were poorly coordinated with other decision makers in Ankara. The result was that Turkish policies tended to be a compromise between Özal's visions, and the limitations and corrections imposed by Turkey's international situation, plus the demands of other actors in the Turkish government.

As Nicole and Hugh Pope remark, the crisis caused by Saddam Hussein's invasion of Kuwait was 'a godsend for Turgut Özal', since it enabled him to deflect attention from his domestic failings at the time, and to inject into foreign policy the dynamism and ambition which had characterised his economic reforms during the 1980s.[13] It also enabled him to demonstrate Turkey's continuing strategic value to the Western powers, in spite of the ending of the cold war. Apparently, he hoped that full support for the Western powers in the crisis would strengthen Turkey's case for gaining eventual accession to the EU, and that Turkey would be able to play an important role in the post-war security of the Gulf. However, it is not fully clear how he intended to achieve this. Inevitably, policies were formulated in accordance with the expectations at the time, which were not always borne out. In particular, it appears that by the late autumn of 1990, both Özal and President Bush expected that military action to expel the Iraqi forces from Kuwait would be inevitable, and that it would be successful. More crucially, according to a later admission by Bush, they both expected that Iraq's military defeat in Kuwait would bring about the overthrow of Saddam Hussein by his own people, and hence a radical change in the Middle Eastern political system as a whole.[14] Özal's actual and attempted policies towards Iraq during the crisis have to be seen in the light of this unrealized expectation, which also helps to explain some of his more controversial ambitions. Throughout, however, Özal seems to have believed that there was complementarity between Turkey's national interests and the policies of the United States. Since it was assumed that the Western coalition would win a war against Iraq, Turkey could best promote those interests by working with Washington, rather than independently. Turkey must also play an active part in helping to deal with the crisis. As he told the opening meeting of the Turkish parliament on 1 September 1990:

> We should not turn a blind eye to events which could occur in the region during the crisis, or the negative effects on our country of potential changes which could emerge after the crisis. Hence, we should apply a dynamic foreign policy, so as to arrive at a position which will ensure that we have an effective [influence] over these developments and changes ... Otherwise, we will obviously lose the chance of becoming an influential country in a situation involving Turkey's vital interests.[15]

It appears that, some months before the fatal events of August 1990, Özal warned President Bush that Saddam Hussein would be a serious danger, and that he might invade Kuwait. By late July, the Iraqi dictator was massing his forces on his border with Kuwait, suggesting that an invasion was imminent. However, on 27 July Bush informed Özal that the Egyptian President Hosni Mubarak had assured him that Saddam would withdraw his forces without mounting an invasion, and that this was confirmed by intelligence reports from the US embassy in Baghdad. On 1 August, at Bush's suggestion, Özal left Ankara for what turned out to be a brief holiday. The following day, when the invasion was reported, he quickly returned to the capital with his advisers, and immediately called a meeting of the National Security Council (NSC), bringing together the President, Prime Minister, other government ministers, and the armed forces chiefs.[16]

Initially, and in spite of Özal's later decision to adopt a more active policy, the government's reaction was hesitant. At meetings of the cabinet and the NSC between 2 and 6 August it was decided to take a 'wait and see' attitude. Meanwhile, on 5 August, Taha Yassin Ramadan, the Deputy Prime Minister of Iraq, visited Ankara and tried to persuade Özal that Turkey should oppose the expected economic embargo on Iraq. Özal was unmoved, urging that Saddam should immediately withdraw from Kuwait, and warning of the consequences to Iraq if he failed to do so. On the following day (6 August) the UN Security Council passed Resolution 661, imposing an economic embargo on Iraq until it withdrew from Kuwait. This prompted a positive response from Ankara two days later, when Özal 'officially' announced on British and US television that the Kirkuk–Yumurtalık pipeline had been closed, and an embargo on trade with Iraq was applied.[17]

The main events between then and the opening of the offensive against Iraq on 17 January 1991 can be quickly summarized. As the likelihood of a war between Iraq and the coalition powers (essentially, the US) became ever stronger, it became apparent that the Bush administration would make three main requests to Turkey, apart from the maintenance of the economic embargo against Iraq; first, the use of air-bases on Turkish soil for attacks on northern Iraq; secondly, a build-up of Turkish forces along the Iraqi–Turkish frontier, so as to draw part of the Iraqi army away from the southern front; thirdly, the participation of a Turkish contingent in the coalition forces which were expected to be fighting in the Gulf.[18] All these demands ran quite contrary to Turkey's previous neutrality in Middle Eastern conflicts, but changes had been made inevitable by the fact that Saddam Hussein had broken the rules of the game, and Western military intervention, with United Nations endorsement, seemed inevitable. If he had been able to decide policy purely by himself, Özal would have been happy to accept all three conditions, and maybe more: as it was, he was only able to apply the first two.

Article 92 of the Turkish constitution requires the passage of a special resolution by parliament to allow the government to declare a state of war, to send Turkish forces abroad, or receive foreign forces on Turkish soil, unless this is required by 'international treaties to which Turkey is a party [in effect, the North Atlantic Treaty] or by the rules of international courtesy'. Neither of the last two conditions applied in this case. If parliament is not in session, then the President can 'decide on the use of the Turkish Armed Forces' by himself, but only if Turkey is subjected to 'sudden armed aggression'. On 12 August the National Assembly was hastily reconvened, and Prime Minister Yıldırım Akbulut asked for these powers. However, the government faced serious objections, not only from the opposition parties, but also an important part of the ruling Motherland Party's parliamentary group, led by former Foreign Minister Mesut Yılmaz.[19] This reflected strong public reluctance to allow Turkey to get involved in a war in the Middle East. Accordingly, parliament voted through the resolution, but with the rider that the government could only exercise these powers if Turkey were attacked. This left the government with no more powers than it would have had anyway during the parliamentary recess, and with no authorization to take pre-emptive moves against Iraq. On 5 September, after parliament had reconvened for its normal autumn session, Akbulut repeated the government's demand for special powers under Article 92. This time, the motion was passed, but, according to Akbulut, the government would only have been able to send Turkish troops abroad if Turkey had been attacked.[20] Hence, parliamentary opposition to direct involvement in a war in the Gulf had been made clear.

The probability of such a war loomed closer during the following two months, as the US built up its forces in the Gulf to around 400,000, and Saddam showed no signs of withdrawing from Kuwait. On 29 November, the UN Security Council adopted Resolution 678, effectively authorizing the US-led coalition to launch military action against Iraq if it failed to withdraw by 15 January 1991. Meanwhile, Turkey increased its forces along the frontier with Iraq to around 120,000 troops, and the US sent a detachment of Patriot missiles to the main NATO air base at İncirlik, near Adana, to improve the Turks' inadequate air defences.

The air war against Iraq began on 17 January. On the same day, the Turkish parliament passed its own Resolution 126, drafted by the government, 'to support UN Security Council Resolution 678' – in effect, to allow coalition air forces to use İncirlik and other bases in Turkey for offensive operations against Iraq.[21] These duly began on 18 January 1991.

Apart from the problems which the government faced in persuading parliament to support the coalition campaign, it is clear that there was also widespread resentment of Özal's tendency to take matters into his own hands, and short-circuit the normal procedures. Numerous examples of this came to light. At the very beginning of the crisis, his announcement of 7 August that the Kirkuk–Yumurtalık pipeline was being closed was made without any previous consultation with the Prime Minister or Foreign Minister, who were only informed about the decision after it had been made public. Similarly, his discussions with the Iraqi deputy premier on 5 August, and with US Secretary of State James Baker, who visited Ankara several times during the crisis, were conducted solo by the President. A more public row erupted at the end of September, when Özal visited Washington for talks with President Bush, but without his Foreign Minister Ali Bozer. This provoked Bozer's resignation on 11 October 1990, to be followed by that of the Defence Minister, Safa Giray, seven days later, and finally, and most startlingly, that of General Necip Torumtay, the Chief of the General Staff, on 3 December.[22] Disputes continued up to the start of the Gulf war. As Akbulut relates, Özal argued that it would not be necessary to go to parliament for a special resolution to allow coalition air forces to use Turkish bases for attacks on Iraq, but the Prime Minister successfully overruled him on this.[23]

General Torumtay's resignation caused a considerable stir, partly because the abrupt departure of the top commander of the armed forces is a rare event in Turkey, and partly because he had been Özal's own choice for the job, against the preferences of the military establishment, in 1987. In his resignation statement, Torumtay explained rather cryptically that he had left his command 'because I see it as impossible to continue my service under the principles and perception of the state which I believe in'.[24] However, it later became clear that his resignation did not simply derive from the fact that he had been cut out of the decision-making loop, but from real policy differences with Özal over Turkey's reaction to the crisis. His reservations were apparently shared by several members of the government, including the Prime Minister. The first bone of contention was Özal's desire to send a detachment of Turkish troops to the Gulf, to join the coalition forces lining up against Iraq. In a television interview in January 1991, Özal confirmed that he had wanted to do this.[25] On his side, Torumtay later related that the government did not give any specific orders to that effect, but that Özal simply floated the idea, and that the likely gains and losses were evaluated by the Foreign Ministry and General Staff (to what effect is unclear).[26] Although one cannot be sure of the details, the conclusion is that Özal certainly wanted to send Turkish troops to the Gulf, but the idea was turned down by the military and Foreign Service chiefs, as well as the cabinet.

A more controversial claim by Necip Torumtay is that Özal wished to open up a 'second front' against Iraq, by launching a land invasion of the north of the country if the coalition was involved in military action in the south, with the objective of capturing and occupying Mosul and Kirkuk. According to Güneş Taner, who by this stage was a Minister of State in Akbulut's government, 'Özal wanted a second front, to be at the "table of the wolves" when they were dividing the spoils after the battle', although he personally opposed the idea.[27] Torumtay's claim is also confirmed by Yıldırım Akbulut and Hüsnü Doğan, who succeeded Safa Giray as Minister of Defence.[28]

In his memoirs and subsequent statements, Torumtay makes it clear that he strongly opposed any such operation. If Turkey occupied Mosul, then it would be as guilty as Saddam of occupying the territory of a foreign country. This would be opposed by the United Nations, which would force Turkey to withdraw, leaving it with no gains. Militarily, the Turkish forces would have been capable of capturing Mosul, he judged, but occupying the region on a long-term basis would have been a different matter. The Kurds of the region would have mounted resistance, worsening the problem which Turkey already faced in fighting the PKK. Preparing for such an operation would have taken as long as three months, but since the idea was only broached by Özal at the end of November 1990, the time was unavailable. It would also have meant reducing Turkey's defences against the USSR, opening up other dangers. Finally, Torumtay strongly objected to the way the proposal was delivered. Two days before his resignation, Özal had sent him a 'directive' (presumably about his plans for operations in northern Iraq) but this had not been discussed or signed by the cabinet, and ignored the fact that he had to take his orders from the government, not the President. This short-circuiting of the constitutional procedures was evidently the straw which broke the camel's back for Torumtay.[29] Significantly, it is clear that Akbulut and his government also opposed the idea of an operation in northern Iraq, undermining the common notion that the Prime Minister was no more than Özal's puppet.[30]

Against this, some commentators argue that Özal did not intend to launch a military operation in northern Iraq, and had no designs on the Mosul province. In an interview in *Tercüman* newspaper, published on 8 December 1990, Özal dismissed the idea for some of the same reasons as those advanced by Torumtay – that the major powers would never permit it, and it would upset the regional balance of power.[31] This message was repeated in an interview with the German newspaper *Die Welt*, published on 22 February 1991, in which Özal stated categorically that 'we will not enter the war so long as we are not attacked by Iraq. We are not thinking of taking even a centimetre of Iraq's territory. Will Turkey take Mosul and Kirkuk? No, it will not.'[32] In a separate conversation with the Turkish journalist Cengiz Çandar, he also pointed to the probable opposition of neighbouring states (presumably, Syria and Iran) if Turkey tried to take over any part of Iraq.[33] Nor is there any certain or direct evidence that President Bush asked Özal to open a 'second front' in the land war against Iraq, although Özal did get permission from Bush to send Turkish forces into Iraq if either Saddam, Syria or Iran invaded Turkey.[34] It is hard to see how Özal could have ignored this obstacle without losing the rest of his broad policy objectives.

To explain this apparently contradictory evidence, two proposals can be advanced. The first would be that, during the November and early December of 1990, Özal did seriously consider a Turkish invasion of northern Iraq with the occupation of Mosul and Kirkuk, if a Gulf war broke out, but then abandoned the idea, in view of the objections raised by Torumtay and others.

The second derives from Özal's apparent expectation that Saddam would be defeated in Kuwait, and would then be overthrown in his own country. In fact, it appears that after Iraqi forces had been ejected from Kuwait, he urged President Bush to order an advance on Baghdad, as well as support for the Kurdish rebellion in Iraq. This, he hoped, would bring about Saddam's overthrow, and the establishment of a democratic government in Iraq which could settle Baghdad's problems with the Kurds and re-establish a stable and friendly relationship with Turkey.[35] On the other hand, if no successor regime were established, there could be a power vacuum in Iraq, in which one of its other neighbours could intervene, or the Iraqi Kurds might try to establish an independent state, either by themselves or with the help of another government. This was regarded as anathema by the Turks. As Özal claimed in his interview with *Die Welt*, a Turkish military intervention might be necessary to prevent this. For Iraq, and for the Iraqi Kurds, the best solution would be a democratic regime in which its different ethnic and religious communities could coexist.[36] The journalist Cengiz Çandar confirms this by relating that Özal told him in January 1991 that if Iraq fell apart after the war, then Turkey should act to prevent Iran or Syria from filling the power vacuum in the north of the country. Even if Iraq did not disintegrate,

> then it will have a new power structure, it will not be the
> old Iraq ... I must establish what sort of Iraq it should be,
> since it is my neighbour and I have security problems ...
> At this testing time, I must be on the inside, I must be
> active, so that I can have my say.[37]

The fact that this idea was advanced without officially abandoning

Turkey's traditional claim that it wished to preserve the territorial integrity of Iraq suggests that Özal did not expect that a Turkish military presence in the country, if it happened, would be more than temporary, pending the establishment of a new political order in Iraq which would meet Turkish objectives.

Turkey, the Kurds and Iraq: January 1991–April 1993

Between 17 January and the middle of March 1991 events proceeded much as expected. The coalition air forces made regular use of İncirlik and other bases in Turkey to attack targets in northern Iraq, and Turkey's military build-up along its frontier with Iraq pinned down about eight Iraqi divisions which could otherwise have been used against coalition forces in the south. The coalition ground offensive began on 24 February, the Iraqi forces were ejected from Kuwait, and on 3 March the two sides agreed to end hostilities. Hence, as Turgut Özal stressed in a television broadcast on 2 March, Turkey appeared to have come out of the war with flying colours.[38] It had helped to prove its importance to the West in the post-cold war world, and had played a positive role in defeating Saddam, without itself firing a shot in anger. It had greatly strengthened its relationship with Washington, where President Bush was warmly appreciative of Özal's support and leadership of his country.[39]

After the war, however, the crisis developed dimensions which neither President Bush nor President Özal had expected. On 15 February, George Bush had issued an open call for rebellion in Iraq, saying that 'The Iraqi military and the Iraqi people [should] take matters into their own hands and force Saddam Hussein the dictator to step aside.'[40] However, he failed to back this up by giving any material support to a rebellion. Contrary to the predictions of both Bush and Özal, Saddam was not overthrown, and when rebellions broke out led by the Shi'ite opposition in the south of Iraq, and in Iraqi Kurdistan, he had enough remaining forces to repress them savagely. In the latter case, Saddam's counter-offensive drove around 500,000 destitute refugees to the Turkish border at the beginning of April, with an even bigger number fleeing to Iran. As Özal admitted on 9 April, 'The Gulf War has confirmed that even if wars solve problems, they also often create new ones.'[41] The Turkish government did not want to admit the refugees into Turkish territory, since, as Özal put it, 'we do not want another Palestinian camp on our border',[42] and because their presence would inevitably have exacerbated Turkey's own internal Kurdish problem. On the other hand, it could not ignore their desperate plight, which was shown nightly on the world's TV screens. Between 2 and 9 April, when the first foreign relief supplies arrived, Turkish official bodies and local people supplied thousands of tons of food, clothing and medical equipment to the refugees, and continued this effort after supplies started to arrive from the rest of the world.

However, this clearly offered no long-term solution to the problem. According to his own account, on 2 April Özal telephoned Secretary of State James Baker about the crisis, and Turkey was instrumental in the passage of UN Security Council Resolution 688 three days later. Among other things, this required Iraq to allow 'immediate access by international humanitarian organizations to all those in need of assistance in all parts of Iraq'. On 15 April Özal called President Bush, and urged that 'As a first step these people should be temporarily settled in suitable flat areas in Iraq, near the Turkish border, until security is provided.'[43] Following an initiative originating from the British Prime Minister John Major, Özal's original idea of a limited security zone was expanded into that of establishing a larger 'safe haven' which would allow all the refugees to return to their homes. Accordingly, on 17 April, the coalition powers launched what became known as 'Operation Provide Comfort', under which an international force of 20,000 troops was established at Silopi, near the border with Iraq, and the 'safe haven' was established in the north-east of the country. This allowed virtually all the refugees to return to their homes by the end of May. From July 1991 coalition air forces, based at İncirlik, enforced a no-fly zone in northern Iraq, as far south as the 36th parallel. This prevented Saddam's forces from entering the Kurdish area. The İncirlik operations were dependent on special permission from the Turkish parliament which had to be regularly renewed, normally at six-month intervals.[44]

'Operation Provide Comfort' was successful in solving the immediate refugee crisis, but it also raised several serious problems for Turkey. In the first place, the creation of the safe haven, outside the control of the Iraqi government, went against the firm Turkish principle that the territorial integrity of Iraq must be preserved. Officially, the Iraqi Kurdish leadership was committed to the idea of obtaining autonomy within Iraq, but there was a recurrent Turkish fear that, freed from Baghdad, they would convert this into 'statehood by stealth'.[45] Frequently, this broadened itself in Turkish minds into what was known as the 'Sèvres syndrome' – the fear that the Western powers were supporting a de facto Kurdish state in northern Iraq as a first step towards the territorial break up of Turkey, with the detachment of the Kurdish-inhabited south-east, just as the entente powers of the First World War had tried to do with the abortive Treaty of Sèvres of 1920 (see p. 12).[46] Even if these fears were exaggerated, the power vacuum in northern Iraq certainly allowed the PKK to establish bases there, from which it could attack targets in Turkey, much as it had done during the Iran–Iraq war.

For Özal, also, the outcome of the crisis had a significant effect in inducing him to reverse one of the previous ground-rules of Turkish policy, that Turkey would maintain no contacts with the Iraqi Kurds. The reasons for this change in policy were clear enough. Like it or not, the KDP and PUK were now the effective power-holders in north-eastern Iraq, and Turkey had to deal with them. Moreover, Turkey and the Iraqi Kurdish leaders had mutual security interests. On their side, the Iraqi Kurds were dependent on Turkey for essential supplies, and for maintenance of the 'Provide Comfort' operation which provided vital relief assistance and kept Saddam Hussein's forces out of northern Iraq. In effect, Turkey was the essential middleman in their links with the USA, their main protector. On the other side, Turkey needed access to first-hand information about what was going on in the region and, above all, wanted to prevent the PKK from operating from bases in Iraqi territory. Given that Turkey could not take over direct control of northern Iraq, these objectives could only be met by establishing a working relationship with the Kurdish leaders who, it was correctly assumed, would not necessarily see eye-to-eye with Abdullah Öcalan and his followers.

According to Cengiz Çandar, who evidently played an important role as an intermediary, Özal first raised the possibility of striking up contact with the Iraqi Kurdish leadership in February 1991, while the war in the Gulf was still raging. About two weeks later Çandar met Jelal Talabani and Muhsin Dizayi, a representative of Massoud Barzani, in London. Talabani asked him whether a meeting could be arranged with himself, Barzani and Özal. This led to a visit to Ankara by Talabani and Dizayi on 10–11 March, in which they talked with officials of the foreign ministry, although not to the President himself.[47] Significantly, these contacts took place before the eruption of the refugee crisis or the establishment of 'Operation Provide Comfort'. At this stage, Özal was evidently very cautious, since he only admitted that the visit had taken place some days later, pointing out that 'everyone else is talking to them, why not us? We must be friends with them as much as possible.'[48] However, he had a direct encounter with Talabani in June 1991, when the PUK leader paid a visit to Istanbul for a meeting of the Socialist International, and then went on to Ankara. In early August 1991 a crisis erupted between the two sides, when a PKK gang killed nine Turkish gendarmes stationed at Samanlı, in the remote province of Hakkari, and carried off another seven to their base in Iraq. In response, Turkish ground and air forces launched a counter-attack which lasted until 19 August. This caused damage to Kurdish villages loyal to the KDP, provoking complaints from Barzani, but left the PKK relatively unscathed.[49] Meanwhile, Talabani and Dizayi returned to Ankara, evidently trying to end the attacks as soon as possible so as to prevent further civilian casualties, and to secure food and other supplies from Turkey. However, it was noticed that they did not publicly condemn the Turkish operation, and undertook to prevent the PKK from launching further raids from their territory. In effect, they appeared willing to trade material assistance for a common front against the PKK.

In October 1991 changes in domestic politics began to have

an effect on Turkish foreign policy, as the Motherland Party was defeated in early general elections. This led to the formation of a coalition government headed by Özal's old rival, Süleyman Demirel, who had served as Prime Minister in four governments during the 1960s and 1970s, but had been excluded from politics by the military regime of 1980–3, until 1987. Demirel's partner in the coalition was the Social Democrat Populist Party (SHP), successor to the Republican People's Party (CHP), and led by İsmet İnönü's son, Erdal İnönü. From this time on, Özal lost much of his domestic power base, and began to act almost as though he was part of the opposition rather than of the government. In his policy approaches, Demirel was more conservative than Özal, but could not prevent him from pursuing his own initiatives.

Nonetheless, the contacts with the Iraqi Kurds which Özal had established continued to develop. Within Iraq, the KDP and PUK established what was known as the 'Kurdish Regional Government' (KRG) based in Arbil in July 1992. This naturally provoked strong suspicions on the Turkish side that the two organizations were on their way to establishing an independent Kurdistan, although neither Talabani nor Barzani participated directly in the KRG, setting up separate zones of control in the south and north of the region respectively.[50] To gain regional support, Turkey organized a meeting in November 1992 with Iranian and Syrian representatives, declaring joint opposition to establishment of a Kurdish state. This was confirmed at a meeting of the three countries' representatives in Damascus in August 1993, with further meetings continuing into 1995.[51] Meanwhile, Turkey granted Turkish diplomatic passports to the two Iraqi Kurdish leaders, and later allowed them to open representative offices in Ankara.[52] Moreover, relations with the KDP improved markedly during the summer and autumn of 1992, after the PKK halted the flow of trucks across south-eastern Turkey into Iraqi Kurdistan, prompting the KDP to demand the withdrawal of PKK units from Iraqi territory. During October and November the Turkish armed forces joined the *peshmergas* of the Iraqi Kurds in a campaign against the PKK, after which its presence in Iraq was moved to a camp at Zalah, on the Iran–Iraq border, and about 130 km south of the frontier with Turkey. In late December General Esref Bitlis, the commander of the Turkish gendarmerie, reached an agreement with Talabani and Barzani which provided that, in return for a Turkish withdrawal, a chain of police posts would be built along the border, and that the *peshmergas* would cooperate in preventing the PKK from penetrating into Turkey. This was not entirely effective, however, as it did not prevent the PKK returning to the border areas in 1993.[53]

In the course of a visit to Ankara in July 1992, Jelal Talabani tried to develop his relationship with Turkey by suggesting that Iraqi Kurdistan might be brought under Turkish protection, or even that it might federate with Turkey. As he put it at the time,

> either we become a part of Iraq or a part of another Middle Eastern government ... The Kurdish people will look for the best possibilities ... We think that in this turning point of history there is a very good historical chance to revive the historical relations between the Kurdish people and the Turkish people.[54]

According to Kaya Toperi, Özal's adviser, Talabani had earlier suggested that if the Kurds set up an autonomous administration in Iraqi Kurdistan, then Turkey might annex it, and asked Özal 'are you our elder brother?' (read 'protector'). This was apparently connected in Talabani's mind to the belief that Özal favoured some sort of federal structure within Turkey itself, although he does not make clear whether he thought Iraqi Kurdistan should be part of this.[55] The proposal can be seen as part of Özal's contemporary conversion to the idea that Turkey should abandon the commitment to monolithic Turkish ethnic nationalism, opting instead for a pluralistic, multi-cultural identity, which would embrace the Kurds and other ethnic groups.[56] However, later commentators like Ertuğrul Özkök argue that Özal never seriously adopted the idea of a federal structure for Turkey, but simply suggested that the idea should be discussed. On the question of a federal relationship with Iraqi Kurdistan, Kaya Toperi categorically denies that Özal approved of the project.[57]

Apart from the establishment of 'Operation Provide Comfort' and of relations with the Iraqi Kurds, the most significant effect of the Gulf crisis of 1990–1 was economic. As already noticed, Iraq had been one of Turkey's most important trade partners in the 1980s. Transport and trade across the Iraqi frontier had also been an important source of income and employment in the impoverished provinces of south-eastern Turkey, most of whose inhabitants were ethnic Kurds. Hence, the imposition of sanctions against Iraq was very costly for Turkey, both nationally and locally. Estimates made by the writer at the time suggested that the cost to Turkey's balance of payments, caused by lost exports, pipeline royalties, and other invisibles, was around US$2 billion per year, although other estimates put the loss at far higher than this.[58] In return, Turkey received compensation aid from Saudi Arabia and Kuwait of around US$2.2 billion in 1991, tailing off to around US$900

million in 1992, and apparently ceasing thereafter.[59] The substantial
net loss to Turkey is sometimes cited as a criticism of Özal's policy
during the Gulf crisis.[60] On the other hand, it has to be remembered
that Turkey could not have ignored a mandatory decision by the
UN Security Council, and that the application of sanctions would
almost certainly have been inevitable, regardless of whatever other
policies Özal might have adopted during the crisis.

Assessments and Implications

During the last months of his life, Turgut Özal was heavily
involved in trying to find a solution to Turkey's internal struggle
against the PKK. He exploited his links with the Iraqi Kurdish
leadership for this purpose, and establishing an indirect channel
of communication with the PKK leader Abdullah Öcalan, via Jelal
Talabani. In a letter to Özal, delivered on 5 March 2003, Talabani
stated that Öcalan had offered to end his campaign of violence in
return for the opening of a 'fraternal dialogue' with the Turkish
government. He claimed that Öcalan had abandoned his previous
goal of establishing an independent Kurdish state, and accepted
'democracy, human rights and cultural and administrative rights
within the unitary Turkish entity'. A passage in the letter also
suggests that Talabani had previously acted as intermediary in
indirect negotiations between Öcalan and Özal, in which Özal had
put forward proposals which had then been rejected by Öcalan.[61]
On 17 March Öcalan announced that his organization would
declare a unilateral ceasefire between 20 March and 15 April. This
was largely observed, and on 16 April the PKK leader went further
by announcing that the ceasefire would be extended indefinitely.
Coincidentally, Özal died of a heart attack on the following day

(17 April). Meanwhile, Öcalan's move left the government in a state of indecision. Its attentions were diverted by the need to elect a new President, which caused Demirel's resignation as Prime Minister on 23 April, his election as President on 16 May, and the appointment of Tansu Çiller as Turkey's first woman Prime Minister and the leader of Demirel's True Path Party on 13 June. As a result, the government missed the chance to end the PKK's campaign. This prospect vanished over the horizon on 24 May when a gang under the command of Semdin Sakık, the PKK's local commander in Bingöl province, attacked a bus carrying unarmed soldiers and civilians, killing thirty-one soldiers and six civilians in cold blood. As a result, military action against the PKK was resumed at full scale.[62]

This, and the economic costs of the sanctions campaign against Iraq, were not the only setbacks Turkey encountered after Özal's apparently successful policies during the Gulf war of 1991. His hope that supporting the West against Saddam Hussein would strengthen Turkey's chances of gaining admission to the European Union proved to be quite misplaced, since most of the EU member states put more weight on Turkey's poor human rights record, and such issues as the budgetary costs of Turkish membership, than its strategic role in the Middle East. In fact, in the years that followed, Turkey was specifically excluded from the list of candidate countries by the meeting in Luxembourg of the European Council in 1997. This decision was not reversed until December 1999. Özal had also hoped that, after Saddam's defeat in Kuwait, Turkey could play an important role in long-term security arrangements between the Gulf states, the US and Turkey. This failed to materialize, since the Gulf states were too weak and divided to make the project work.

Accordingly, the US effectively took over the role of trying to maintain Gulf security, with Turkey left on the sidelines.[63]

The Gulf crisis had created a classic dilemma for Turkish policy makers, of reconciling internal with external political pressures. On the one hand, domestic opinion strongly favoured the continuation of the previous policy of non-intervention in Middle Eastern conflicts. On the other hand, Turkey's links with the United States and its obligations to the United Nations, made this virtually impossible to continue. This dilemma repeated itself, in even more striking form, when a similar crisis erupted in 2002–3, albeit with quite different results.

Assessing Özal's policies during the Gulf crisis is also difficult since, as has been seen, there are several uncertainties in the story, and conflicting testimonies. It seems clear, however, that Özal tried to have Turkey play a far more active part in the war than it actually achieved – in particular, that he wanted Turkish troops to participate in the coalition force in the south and, quite probably, to open a 'northern front' against Iraq from Turkish territory. Both these proposals ran contrary to some of the basic assumptions underlying Turkish policy to Iraq outlined earlier (pp. 25–6). In particular, the proposal that Turkish troops should occupy Mosul and Kirkuk bluntly contradicted Turkey's oft-repeated claim that it wished to protect the territorial integrity of Iraq (implicitly, to prevent the establishment of an independent Kurdish state) as well as its treaty obligations to respect the established frontier, dating back to 1926. Özal's proposals were left on the shelf, partly because of these political objections, and partly because of the military problems a Turkish occupation of northern Iraq would have created. In effect, most of the old rules re-established themselves, in spite of Özal's ambitions (such as they may have been). At the same time, while Özal won warm plaudits from the United States for his policies, these failed to translate themselves into domestic support. Looking back on the story, many Turks became convinced that their country had gained nothing by supporting the coalition, as its economy had been harmed and the campaign by the PKK continued unabated for several years. This reaction ignored the vital US support which Turkey received in two later economic crises, in 1994 and 2001, as well as Washington's consistent support for Turkey's membership of the European Union, both of which were largely based on its perceived strategic importance to the West in the Gulf war of 1991. Nevertheless, it was quite firmly and commonly held. All these considerations were to have important effects when a new Gulf war erupted twelve years later.[64]

After 1991, the main problem for Turkey in determining its policy towards Iraq was not that Iraq was too strong, but that it was too weak – in particular that its government did not control all its own territory. The main change produced by the Gulf war of 1991 was the creation of what was virtually an autonomous Kurdish state in Iraq. This was an outcome which neither Turkey nor the US had originally planned, but which was forced on them as the only practical solution to the refugee crisis of April 1991. Again, this ran quite contrary to previous Turkish assumptions, which strongly opposed any actual or incipient partition of Iraqi territory, or any contact with the Iraqi Kurdish leadership. Since it was not in Turkey's power to restore the pre-war situation, Özal and his successors had to cope with realities – in particular, the need to prevent the PKK from using northern Iraq as a base for attacks on Turkish targets. How they tried to do this is outlined in the following chapter.

Notes

1. Quoted, Nicole and Hugh Pope, *Turkey Unveiled: Ataturk and After*, London: John Murray, 1997, p. 165.
2. Although, it may be noted, Korkut Özal had serious differences with Erbakan after the party's disappointing performance in the general elections of 1977. Whether this had any effect on Turgut Özal's later decision to form his own party is uncertain. See Fulya Atacan, 'Explaining Religious Politics at the Crossroad: AKP-SP', *Turkish Studies*, vol. 6, no. 2, 2005, p. 191.
3. See, for instance, his statement at a press conference of 9 March 1989, quoted at length in Hasan Cemal, *Özal Hikayesi*, Ankara and Istanbul: Bilgi, 1989, pp. 161–2, and M. Sait Yazıcıoğlu, 'Özal'ın İslam Anlayışı ve Dini Özgürlükler', in İhsan Sezal and İhsan Dağı, eds, *Özal: Siyaset, İktisat, Zihniyet*, Istanbul: Boyut, 2001, esp. pp. 203–4.
4. See Berdal Aral, 'Dispensing with Tradition? Turkish Politics and International Society during the Özal Decade', *Middle Eastern Studies*, vol. 37, no. 1, 2001, pp. 73–7.
5. See Henri J. Barkey, 'The Silent Victor: Turkey's Role in the Gulf War', in Efraim Karsh, ed., *The Iran–Iraq War: Impact and Implications*, London: Macmillan, in association with Jafee Center for Strategic Studies, Tel Aviv University, 1989, pp. 135–40 and Philip Robins, *Turkey and the Middle East*, London: Pinter, for Royal Institute of International Affairs, 1991, pp. 53–4, 58–62 and 103.
6. Data from *Statistical Yearbook of Turkey*, Ankara: State Institute of Statistics, for 1981, 1987, and 1993.
7. Suha Bölükbaşı, 'Turkey Challenges Iraq and Syria: the Euphrates Dispute', *Journal of South Asian and Middle Eastern Studies*, vol. 16, no. 4, 1993, pp. 22–3. For Iraq, the Euphrates is less important as a source of water than the Tigris, which was unaffected by the Ataturk dam. According to Turkish figures, Iraq draws about four times as much water from the Tigris and its tributaries, 90 per cent of which flows directly from Turkey into Iraq, as it does from the Euphrates. See Lenore G. Martin, 'Turkey's Middle East Foreign Policy', in Lenore G. Martin and Dimitris Keridis, eds, *The Future of Turkish Foreign Policy*, Cambridge MA and London: MIT Press, 2004, p. 171.
8. Following his defeat in 1975 (see p. 24) Mustafa Barzani had gone into exile, and died in the United States in 1979.
9. Charles Tripp, *A History of Iraq*, Cambridge: Cambridge University Press, 2000, pp. 243–4. Talabani had originally broken away from the KDP, to form the PUK, in 1975. For further information on the PKK's campaign during the 1980s, see David McDowall, *A Modern History of the Kurds*, London: I. B. Tauris, 1996, pp. 418–31; Michael M. Gunter, *The Kurds in Turkey*, Boulder, CO: Westview, 1990, pp. 57–91, and Kemal Kirişçi and Gareth Winrow, *The Kurdish Question and Turkey: an Example of Trans-state Ethnic*

Conflict, London: Cass, 1997, pp. 126–36.

10. Melek Firat and Ömer Kürkçüoğlu, 'Arap Devletleriyle İlişkiler', in Baskın Oran, ed., *Türk Dış Politikası: Kurtuluş Savaşından Bügüne: Olgular, Belgeler, Yorumlar*, vol. 2, Istanbul: İletişim, 2001, pp. 133–6.

11. Ibid. pp. 138–9; McDowall, *Modern History*, pp. 357–61.

12. Statement by Güneş Taner, in Mehmet Ali Birand and Soner Yalçın, eds, *The Özal: Bir Davanın Öyküsü*, Istanbul: Doğan, 2001, pp. 435–6.

13. Nicole and Hugh Pope, *Turkey Unveiled*, p. 218.

14. Statement by George Bush Snr, in Birand and Yalçın, eds, *The Özal*, p. 427. President Bush adds that this expectation was shared by the French President François Mitterand, the Egyptian President Hosni Mubarak and 'all the Arab leaders'. He also states that he had never expected Saddam to be so ruthless in suppressing the internal rebellions after his defeat in Kuwait (ibid. p. 448).

15. Quoted, Ramazan Gözen, 'Küzey Irak Sorunu', in İdris Bal, ed., *21 Yüzyılın Eşiğinde Türk Dış Politikası*, Istanbul: Alfa, 2001, p. 519.

16. Statements by Güneş Taner and Kaya Toperi, in Birand and Yalçın, eds, *The Özal*, pp. 417–19. The exact date of Özal's first warning to Bush is not clear: Taner puts it at January 1990, Toperi at 'three months' before the crisis erupted (i.e. May 1990). President Bush confirms the story, saying that Özal had warned him that Saddam 'could do something mad', but says he could not remember when the warning was issued: ibid. p. 427.

17. Ramazan Gözen, 'Türkiye'nin II Körfez Savaşı Politikası: Aktif Politika ve Sonuçları', in Bal, ed, *Türk Dış Politikası*, p. 470: statement by Kaya Toperi, in Birand and Yalçın, eds, *The Özal*, p. 421.

18. İlhan Üzgel, 'ABD ve NATO'yla İlişkiler' in Oran, ed., *Türk Dış Politikası*, vol. 2, p. 255.

19. Yılmaz had resigned from the government in February 1990, apparently because he resented the frequent intervention in the work of his ministry by the President and other members of the government, but did not leave the Motherland Party: see *Milliyet*, 22 Feb. 1990. He became Prime Minister in June 1991, in succession to Akbulut.

20. Yıldırım Akbulut, statement in Birand and Yalçın, eds, *The Özal*, p. 438.

21. For details, see Üzgel, 'ABD ve NATO', p. 262.

22. Gözen, 'Türkiye'nin', p. 470; Üzgel, 'ABD ve NATO', p. 256. However, Safa Giray's resignation did not apparently have to do with the Gulf crisis, but mainly derived from a dispute with Akbulut over the composition of the Istanbul delegation to the Motherland Party's annual convention, to be held in 1991.

23. Statement by Yıldırım Akbulut, in Birand and Yalçın, eds, *The Özal*, p. 438.

24. Quoted, Necip Torumtay, *Orgeneral Torumtay'ın Anıları*, Istanbul: Milliyet, 1994, p. 130.

25. *Summary of World Broadcasts*, London: BBC, 22 Jan 1991.

26. Torumtay, *Anılar*, p. 112.

27. Quoted, Nicole and Hugh Pope, *Turkey Unveiled*, p. 220.
28. Ibid. pp. 115–16, and statements by Necip Torumtay, Yıldırım Akbulut and Hüsnü Doğan, in Birand and Yalçın, eds, *The Özal*, pp. 422–4, 430–2, 435 and 439. Nicole and Hugh Pope also relate that, in a visit to the Washington Press Club shortly before the Gulf War, Özal 'spent most of the evening briefing correspondents at his table about Turkey's rights to northern Iraq': *Turkey Unveiled*, p. 226.
29. Torumtay, *Anılar*, pp. 115–16, and statements in Birand and Yalçın, eds, *The Özal*, pp. 430–2 and 440–2.
30. Yıldırım Akbulut, statement in Birand and Yalçın, eds, *The Özal*, p. 435.
31. Cited by Gözen, 'Türkiye'nin', pp. 484–5.
32. Quoted, Gözen, 'Küzey Irak', pp. 520–1.
33. Ibid. p. 521.
34. Üzgel, 'ABD ve NATO', p. 257. However, Nicole and Hugh Pope quote Güneş Taner as saying of Özal's plan to open up a second front that 'the Americans were all for it': *Turkey Unveiled*, p. 220. The writer does not know of any clear evidence to confirm this.
35. Nicole and Hugh Pope, *Turkey Unveiled*, p. 228; Mahmut Balı Aykan, 'Turkey's Policy in Northern Iraq, 1991–5', *Middle Eastern Studies*, vol. 32, no. 4, 1996, p. 345.
36. Gözen, 'Küzey Irak', p. 520.
37. Cengiz Çandar, statement in Birand and Yalçın, eds, *The Özal*, p. 460.
38. *Summary of World Boadcasts*, 4 Mar. 1991.
39. Statement by George Bush in Birand and Yalçın, eds, *The Özal*, pp. 426–7.
40. *New York Times*, 16 Feb. 1991: quoted, Michael Rubin, 'The Future of Iraq: Democracy, Civil War or Chaos?', *MERIA Journal*, vol. 9, no. 3, 2005, p. 127.
41. 'President Turgut Özal's Address to the Global Panel sponsored by the European Studies Centre in Amsterdam': text reprinted in *Studies on Turkish–Arab Relations: Special Issue on the Gulf Crisis*, Istanbul: Foundation for Studies on Turkish–Arab Relations, annual, vol. 6, 1991, pp. 206–8. The words quoted are on p. 206.
42. Ibid. p. 207.
43. 'President Özal's TV Speech concerning Turkish Help to Iraqi Refugees' (31 May 1991): text in ibid. pp. 209–11. The passage quoted is on p. 210. For the full text of Resolution 688, see ibid. pp. 185–6.
44. Kemal Kirişçi, 'Turkey and the Kurdish Safe Haven in Northern Iraq', *Journal of South Asian and Middle Eastern Studies*, vol. 19, no. 3, 1996, pp. 21–3, and 'Provide Comfort or Trouble: Operation Provide Comfort and its Impact on Turkish Foreign Policy', *Turkish Review of Middle East Studies*, Istanbul: Ortadoğu ve Balkan İncelemeleri Vakfı, annual vol. 8, 1994/5, pp. 44–51. See also Aykan, 'Turkey's Policy', pp. 345–6. Originally, the relief operation was referred to as 'Operation Provide Comfort', with the İncirlik-based operation known as 'Poised Hammer', but 'Provide Comfort' was later

used as the title for both. From the beginning of 1997 it became known as 'Operation Northern Watch'.

45. Kirişçi, 'Provide Comfort', p. 45.

46. For a broader survey, see Dietrich Jung, 'The Sèvres Syndrome: Turkish Foreign Policy and its Historical Legacies', *American Diplomacy*, vol. 8, no. 2, 2003.

47. Statement by Cengiz Çandar, in Birand and Yalçın, eds, *The Özal*, pp. 458 and 462–3.

48. Quoted, *The Independent*, London, 15 Mar. 1991.

49. *The Guardian*, London and *The Independent*, 14 Aug. 1991; Philip Robins, *Suits and Uniforms: Turkish Foreign Policy since the Cold War*, London: Hurst, 2003, pp. 323–4.

50. Bill Park, *Turkey's Policy towards Northern Iraq: Problems and Perspectives*, London: International Institute for Strategic Studies, Adelphi Paper 374, 2005, p. 20; Charles Tripp, *A History of Iraq*, Cambridge: Cambridge University Press, 2000, p. 272; Robins, *Suits and Uniforms*, p. 325; Kirişçi, 'Turkey and the Kurdish Safe Haven', p. 23; Aykan, 'Turkey's Policy', p. 351.

51. Mahmut Bali Aykan, 'Turkey's Perspectives on Turkish–US Relations concerning Persian Gulf Security in the Post-Cold War Era, 1989–1995', *Middle East Journal*, vol. 50, no. 3, 1996, p. 354; Robert Olson, 'The Kurdish Question and Turkey's Foreign Policy, 1991–1995: From the Gulf War to the Incursion into Iraq', *Journal of South Asian and Middle Eastern Studies*, vol. 19, no. 1, 1995, pp. 5–6.

52. Üzgel, 'ABD ve NATO', p. 263.

53. Hugh Pope, 'Digging into Iraq', *Middle East International*, 27 Nov. 1992; Robins, *Suits and Uniforms*, pp. 326–8; Kirişçi, 'Turkey and the Kurdish Safe Haven', p. 32; Aykan, 'Turkey's Policy', p. 352.

54. Quoted, *Briefing*, Ankara: weekly, 27 July 1992, pp. 4–5.

55. Statements by Kaya Toperi and Jelal Talabani, in Birand and Yalçın, eds, *The Özal*, pp. 456 and 470.

56. See Mühittin Ataman, 'Özal Leadership and the Restructuring of Turkish Ethnic Policy in the 1980s', *Middle Eastern Studies*, vol. 38, no. 4, 2002, esp. pp. 129 and 133.

57. Statements by Ertuğrul Özkök and Toperi Kaya, in Birand and Yalçın, eds, *The Özal*, pp. 455–6 and 470.

58. Estimates by the writer in 1991, for the Economist Intelligence Unit, London. The total was made up as follows: direct exports to Iraq, US$800 million; pipeline royalties, US$300 million; other invisibles (transit trade, contractors' earnings, etc.) US$700–1,000 million. Against this, Ramazan Gözen, for instance, estimates Turkey's total losses between 1990 and 2001 at 'over US$30 billion', or an annual average of around US$3 billion: Gözen, 'Küzey Irak', p. 486.

59. Calculated from Turkish balance of payments figures, in *Briefing*, 27 July

1992, p. 24 and 10 May 1993, pp. 24–5.

60. E.g. by Gözen, 'Küzey Irak', p. 486.

61. The passage reads: 'I put forward to him [Öcalan] my well-known suggestions – those which I had explained to Your Excellency [Özal] in the past and which I brought to him and he rejected at the time.' For what is said to be the full text of the letter, see *Mideast Mirror*, 15 Mar. 1993, p. 23.

62. See Henri J. Barkey and Graham E. Fuller, 'Turkey's Kurdish Question: Critical Turning Points and Missed Opportunities', *Middle East Journal*, vol. 51, no. 1, 1997, p. 70 and Michael M. Gunter, *The Kurds and the Future of Turkey*, New York: St Martin's Press, 1997, pp. 78–80. In his trial in June 1999, Öcalan claimed that he had not ordered the Bingöl attack, and that he had later issued orders for Sakık's murder (*Milliyet*, 2 June 1999). However, his failure to make this clear at the time was a fatal error.

63. Aykan, 'Turkish Perspectives', pp. 348–9.

64. Philip Robins, 'Confusion at Home, Confusion Abroad: Turkey between Copenhagen and Iraq', *International Affairs*, vol. 79, no. 3, 2003, pp. 559–60.

THREE

Turkey, the Kurds and Iraq, 1993–8

The period between 1993 and 1998 marked a transition between the two major Gulf crises of 1991 and 2003. Essentially, Turkey was left with the task of coping with the confused and uncertain situation in Iraq thrown up by the earlier Gulf war, which particularly affected its relations with the Kurds and the United States. Coping with this was made more difficult by serious domestic instability in Turkey, by the rising tide of violence by the PKK, and the failure of successive Turkish governments to deal with the political and economic roots of their internal Kurdish problem.

Domestic Instability and the Kurdish Problem in Turkey

The inconclusive elections of 1991, and the death of Turgut Özal in 1993, set off a period of instability and lack of leadership in Turkish politics which had a damaging effect on both foreign and domestic policies, with weak coalition governments too preoccupied with the basic task of staying in power to develop effective and sustained strategies. After succeeding to the presidency in 1993, Süleyman Demirel tended to adopt a lower profile in day-to-day politics than Özal had done as President, and gradually distanced himself from the True Path Party (DYP) which he had founded. As the new leaders of the DYP and the Motherland Party (Anap) respectively, neither Tansu Çiller nor Mesut Yılmaz had the stature, vision, or experience of their predecessors. On the centre-left, Erdal İnönü, the son of İsmet İnönü, who was leader of the Social Democrat Populist Party (SHP) and Tansu Çiller's partner in the coalition government set up in 1993 (p. 53) had a famous surname, but he was a reluctant politician, and the SHP failed to become a dynamic force in Turkish politics. All the secularist parties were challenged by the rise of the pro-Islamist Welfare Party (*Refah*) led by Necmettin Erbakan, but this played a disruptive role in the system, without promoting effective or generally acceptable alternatives.

The perennial Turkish problem of holding a coalition government together came to the fore in the autumn of 1995. A group of deputies from the SHP led by Deniz Baykal, Bülent Ecevit's main lieutenant in the 1970s, had left the party in 1992 to re-found the Republican People's Party (CHP), which had been dissolved by the then military regime in 1981. This re-united with the SHP in February 1995, under Baykal's leadership and the CHP's title. In the following September Baykal withdrew his party from the coalition and then, after an unsuccessful attempt by Tansu Çiller to form a minority government, agreed to rejoin a temporary coalition with the DYP, but only on condition that general elections be held on 24 December 1995. These caused a shock to the entire secularist establishment, as the Welfare Party emerged from the polls as the biggest party in parliament, with 21.4 per cent of the vote and 158 of the 550 seats. Anap and DYP vied for second place, with 132 and 135 seats respectively, while Bülent Ecevit re-emerged onto the political stage at the head of his own creation, the Democratic Left Party (DSP), capturing seventy-six seats.[1] Deniz Baykal's insistence on early elections turned out to be a chronic miscalculation, as the CHP's parliamentary tally was reduced to forty-nine deputies. Putting together a government in a parliament with no less than five parties, of which the biggest was regarded as quite inimical to all the others, was never going to be easy. After two and a half months of a caretaker government under Tansu Çiller, Mesut Yılmaz formed an uneasy coalition with the DYP on 12 March 1996. This collapsed just one month later, leaving Tansu Çiller to reverse her previously declared hostility to Necmettin Erbakan and all his works by forming a coalition with the Welfare Party, under Erbakan's premiership, and with herself as Foreign Minister, on 26 June 1996.

The 'Refahyol' coalition (as it was known from the contraction of the Turkish titles of its two constituents)[2] was easily the most controversial, as well as the most deeply divided, of Turkey's many governments at this time. Erbakan and Çiller were ideologically poles apart. The DYP was riddled with corruption, while the Welfare Party's Islamist inclinations were hotly opposed by the secularist state establishment as well as much of the public. The long-gestating crisis came out into the open on 28 February 1997 when the National Security Council, which effectively represented the armed forces within the political system, demanded changes in government policy designed to stem creeping Islamism. Erbakan officially accepted these demands, but failed to implement them, and there was a rising tide of public opposition – from business groups, trades unions, women's and human rights organizations – which drew their force as much from the DYP's corruption as opposition to Erbakan's pro-Islamist agenda. On 18 June 1997 Erbakan resigned, hoping to turn over the premiership to Tansu Çiller, but backbench defections from the DYP to a short-lived Democratic Turkey Party (DTP) robbed the government of its majority, and President Demirel passed on the baton to Mesut Yılmaz (as, constitutionally, he was quite entitled to do). Accordingly, Yılmaz formed a minority coalition government with the DTP and Ecevit's DSP, and with uncertain outside support from the CHP. This managed to cling on to office until November 1998 (p. 84). Meanwhile, in February 1998, the Welfare Party was closed down by the Constitutional Court for infringements of articles of the constitution protecting secularism.[3]

While the Islamist challenge was a serious one, the Kurdish question, with an escalating campaign of violence by the PKK, was Turkey's most intractable and damaging problem at the time. Politically, Tansu Çiller followed a wavering line. In January 1995, for instance, she proposed that Ataturk's oft-quoted dictum 'How happy is one who calls himself a Turk' should be changed to 'How happy is one who calls himself a citizen of Turkey',[4] implying a non-ethnic definition of national identity. She was sharply criticized for this, however, and never repeated it. Under her government, political manifestations of Kurdish nationalism were rigidly suppressed, most notably in March 1994, when thirteen deputies of the pro-Kurdish Democracy Party (DEP) who had been elected in 1991 on the SHP ticket, were arrested and charged with treason, and their party closed down (subsequently, six fled abroad, another six were imprisoned, and one murdered).[5] Thereafter, the Kurdish problem was treated as a purely military rather than political one. It was even denied that there was a 'Kurdish problem' at all, but just one of terrorism. Effectively, Tansu Çiller handed over the direction of policy on the issue to the army commanders.[6]

This did not guarantee success, however. In 1993 the PKK's terrorist campaign reached its peak, with Abdullah Öcalan's followers running their own 'liberated zones', extorting taxes from the inhabitants, and conducting massacres of those villagers who opposed them. By 1995 the army was beginning to turn the tide, but it was not until 1998 that it re-established control of most of the Kurdish-inhabited south-eastern provinces.[7] After this, the government turned its attention to Syria, where Öcalan enjoyed the hospitality of the regime as well as logistic support, putting strong diplomatic pressure as well as the threat of military action on Damascus. Bereft of support on this issue from Iran or the other Arab states, Hafiz al-Assad's government expelled Öcalan from Syria on 7 October 1998. He set off on a safari which took him to Italy, Belarus, Russia and Greece, ending up in the Greek ambassador's residence in Nairobi, Kenya in February 1999. Thanks to vital intelligence from the CIA, a Turkish security team abducted him on his way to Nairobi airport on 16 February. He was brought back to Turkey, placed on trial, and condemned to death on 29 June 1999 (this was subsequently commuted to life imprisonment). In August 1999 he effectively admitted defeat, by declaring an indefinite ceasefire, which lasted until September 2003 (p. 131).[8]

Öcalan's arrest and trial caused an upsurge of nationalist sentiment in Turkey, but it was hard to deny that the defeat of the PKK had been bought at a very heavy cost. At the height of the campaign in 1994, between a quarter and a half of the entire manpower of the army (or around 240,000–300,000 troops and police) was reported to be deployed in the south-east, at an estimated cost of up to US$6–7 billion per year.[9] According to official figures released by the Turkish General Staff in March 1999, a total of around 30,000 people had been killed in the fighting, of which 5,600 were Turkish troops and police plus Kurdish militiamen armed by the government and 5,300 were non-combatant civilians, leaving around 19,000 deaths on the PKK side.[10] On official figures, 380,000 people had been driven out of their villages, which in many cases were burned down by the army. Unofficial estimates put the number of internal refugees at three million.[11] Thanks to these draconian tactics, millions of Kurdish citizens had become alienated from the Turkish state. While the PKK had eventually been overcome, no serious attempt had been made to tackle the serious political and economic grievances from which its campaign had drawn its impetus.

Turkey, the US and Israel

Like its counterparts in Western Europe, the US Congress was highly critical of the serious human rights violations which the war against the PKK brought in its train.[12] Turkey could not afford to ignore this criticism, since it was still dependent on the US for economic and military support. The relationship was not entirely one-sided, however, since the United States also needed Turkish support for the maintenance of the 'Provide Comfort' operation which helped to contain Saddam Hussein, and in particular the use of the İncirlik air base, the mandate for which had to be regularly renewed by the Turkish parliament, normally at six-month intervals (p. 50). This permission could not be taken as a foregone conclusion, since 'Provide Comfort' was far from popular in Turkey. This derived primarily from the fear that Turkey might have no control over the allied (mainly US) forces involved and, in particular, that they might indirectly help the PKK – in effect, giving a boost to the 'Sèvres syndrome' among suspicious Turks (p. 50). By keeping Saddam Hussein's forces out of northern Iraq, the operation created a de facto Kurdish state which was likely to encourage Kurdish nationalists in Turkey, as well as providing the PKK with extra-territorial bases.[13] Against this was the argument that Turkey could not afford to oppose the US over a central part of its Middle East policy, and that the force helped to deter Saddam Hussein from attacking Turkey. Had 'Provide Comfort' been ended, leaving the Iraqi army able to resume control over the north of the country, then the Turks would probably have welcomed this, but there was the risk that this would also produce another wave of refugees – the original reason for the start of 'Provide Comfort' in 1991. The second line of argument was consistently supported by the Turkish General Staff and the Foreign Ministry, who carried the day. Hence, although both Süleyman Demirel and Erdal İnönü opposed the operation while in opposition, they both accepted it once they were in government, as did Tansu Çiller in her turn.[14] In spite of their mutual misgivings, both Turkey and the US needed the continuation of 'Provide Comfort'.

In February 1996, Turkey's overall position in Middle Eastern politics entered a new phase when an agreement on military training and cooperation was signed with Israel allowing, among other things, the training of Israeli pilots at Turkish bases, with reciprocal arrangements for the Turkish air force in Israel. This did not come as a bolt from the blue, as it had been preceded by a series of incremental steps strengthening links between Tel Aviv and Ankara since the late 1980s. It was succeeded by a Defence Industry Cooperation Agreement signed in the following August, providing for the upgrading by Israeli firms of Turkey's ageing fleet of 104 Phantom F-4 and F-5 warplanes, and a later deal in 2002 for the modernization of 170 M-60 Turkish tanks, among other projects. For Israel, the entente was important as a means of breaking out of its regional isolation, and gaining training space as well as intelligence sources in Turkey. On the other side, it gave Turkey access to advanced military hardware which was held up by objections from legislatures in the US and Europe, as well as the support of the powerful pro-Israeli lobby in the US Congress. However, the entente fell well short of a full military alliance. Israel was not committed to helping Turkey directly in the struggle against the PKK, or its conflicts with Greece and Cyprus, while Turkey remained neutral in the Arab–Israeli conflict.[15] For Turkey, the rapprochement with Israel was a valuable way of strengthening its ties with the US, but had the disadvantage that, if its relations with Tel Aviv turned sour, this could have a damaging effect on its relationship with Washington, and vice versa, as happened in 2004 (pp. 133–5).

Turkey's relations with the US, Israel and the Western powers generally were put to a severe test during the Refahyol government of 1996–7. The Welfare Party opposed Turkey's bid for membership of the European Union, which Erbakan argued would submerge

Muslim Turkey in a Christian Europe. Hence, in the 1995 election campaign he urged that Turkey should substantially revise the Customs Union agreement which the Çiller government had signed with the EU earlier that year. Similarly, he denounced the 'Provide Comfort' operation as a 'second Sèvres', and strongly opposed the military cooperation agreement with Israel. Once in office, however, Erbakan's bark turned out to be worse than his bite, since he was under strong pressure from both the military and Tansu Çiller (as his Foreign Minister) not to upset Turkey's previous alignments. Hence, he left the Customs Union agreement untouched, while his government renewed the mandate for 'Provide Comfort' in July 1996, and again in the following December (on the second occasion, it was re-named 'Northern Watch', and there were some cosmetic changes, but the operation remained essentially the same). Faced with another démarche from the military, Erbakan reluctantly accepted the agreement with Israel for the Phantom upgrading in August 1996. Shortly before, he had attempted to launch his own initiative when he undertook a five-nation tour of mainly Muslim countries in Asia, followed by visits to Egypt, Libya and Nigeria in October. The Libyan visit turned out to be a fiasco, as Colonel Qaddafi seized the opportunity to launch a fierce public attack on Turkey for its links with Israel, and openly called for the establishment of an independent Kurdish state. While his trips to other countries were less disastrous, Erbakan was left with little to show for his pains. When the Iranian President Akbar Hashemi Rafsanjani visited Turkey in December 1996, Erbakan's attempts to negotiate a defence cooperation agreement with Iran were abruptly terminated by the army chiefs and his own Defence Minister, Turhan Tayan, who was a member of the DYP. If nothing else, the Erbakan experience demonstrated that there was no effective or acceptable 'Islamic' alternative to Turkey's established Western orientation.[16]

Turkey, Iraq and the Iraqi Kurds

Saddam Hussein's political survival after the Gulf war of 1991 left Ankara with the problem of dealing with his government. As a neighbour of Iraq, Turkey could not simply ignore it. In an ideal world, Turkish governments would have liked to see a negotiated settlement between Baghdad and the Kurds, which would have allowed the Iraqi government to resume full control over its national territory, and full compliance by Saddam with UN resolutions demanding the complete removal of Iraq's mass destruction weapons, in return for which the sanctions regime could have been lifted. In fact, in February 1998 the then Foreign Minister İsmail Cem, after consultations with the UN, visited Baghdad with proposals to that effect, with no positive result.[17] Since neither Saddam nor the Iraqi Kurds were willing to meet these conditions, the most Turkey could do was to ensure that the Iraqi dictator would not be actively hostile (for instance, by supporting the PKK) and to try to have the sanctions lifted, or at least eased. After the break in relations caused by the 1991 war, Turkey re-opened its embassy in Baghdad at the level of chargé d'affaires in March–April 1993, being the first NATO country to do so.[18] Although there were occasional reports in the Turkish press that Saddam was aiding the PKK, he rigidly denied this, and there is no clear sign that he gave it more than marginal assistance.[19] On the economic front, the Habur border crossing post between Turkey and Iraq was re-opened for trade in August 1995, with Turkey's exports to Iraq officially limited to food and medicines, in return for fuel from the Kirkuk refinery.[20] Trade relations with Iraq were further expanded after December 1996, when Saddam Hussein finally accepted UN Security Council Resolution 986, allowing Iraq to export oil to the value of US$2 billion per six-month period, 65 per cent of which could be used to buy food and medicines for Iraq. Although this programme was interrupted periodically, as Saddam failed to cooperate with the UN weapons inspectors, it allowed Turkey to partially re-open the Kirkuk–Yumurtalık pipeline, and export goods to Iraq to the tune of around US$500 million per year.[21]

For Turkey, the more problematic relationship was that with the Iraqi Kurds. By 1992 Turkey had established an informal alliance with the KDP and PUK against the PKK (p. 54), although it continued to conduct independent military operations in Iraqi Kurdistan, as in April 1994. Meanwhile, in December 1993 the first armed clashes had broken out between the two Iraqi Kurdish organizations, battling for territory (the KDP in the north, the PUK in the south) and control of customs revenues from the Habur border gate, as well as political leadership of the Kurdish national movement. These intensified in the following May. In December 1994 PUK forces seized Arbil from the KDP, bringing the administration of the region to a halt. This intra-Kurdish civil war caused mixed reactions in Turkey. While it weakened the political case for a Kurdish national state, it also threatened to create chaos in northern Iraq, in which the PKK might gain a free hand. The result was an informal alignment, in which the KDP sided with Turkey, while the PUK allied with the PKK, supported by Iran. Iraqi Kurdistan was effectively divided into three zones, one controlled by the KDP, another by the PUK, and a third small zone by the Islamic Movement of Kurdistan, which had close ties with Iran.[22]

In March 1995 Turkish forces launched another large-scale operation against the PKK, with a reported 35,000 troops, plus tanks and aircraft, which penetrated thirty-five miles into Iraq along a 150-mile front. This was Turkey's biggest military operation in northern Iraq since 1992, the difference from the previous occasion being that while its Kurdish support had previously included both the KDP and PUK, it was now limited to Barzani's organization. The attack caused intense criticism internationally, with the threat that the European Parliament might not ratify the Customs Union agreement with Turkey which was then under negotiation. Nevertheless, it demonstrated the way in which conflict within the Iraqi Kurdish camp had given Turkey a chance to exercise its military muscle, however controversially.[23] Meanwhile, in May 1995, sections of the Turcoman community in northern Iraq set up the Iraqi Turcoman Front, although this was widely suspected as being an instrument of the Turkish government.[24]

By this stage, the Clinton administration was anxious to end the fighting between the PUK and KDP, as part of its ultimately unsuccessful attempt to build up a cohesive and effective internal opposition to Saddam Hussein's regime. To this end, it organized a meeting between the two Kurdish parties in the Irish city of Drogheda on 9–11 August 1995, followed by another round of talks in Dublin on 12–15 September. Turkish representatives attended the talks as observers, and were able to get their security concerns mentioned in the resulting ceasefire agreement. However, Turkey was clearly lukewarm about the idea of regime change by force in Baghdad.[25]

The main defect of the talks in Ireland was that the ceasefire agreement failed to stick. In the summer of 1996, Iranian troops entered Iraqi Kurdistan, allegedly in pursuit of units of the Kurdistan Democratic Party of Iran (KDP-I), which was allied with the Iraqi KDP against the Iranian government. In response, Barzani performed a U-turn, by asking for military support from Baghdad. This came in the form of 30,000 Iraqi troops, who in September 1996 helped the KDP forces to recapture Arbil, going on to take the city of Suleimaniyah from the PUK. Saddam's opponents who had taken refuge in the region were hunted down. Following the withdrawal of Iraqi troops, PUK forces had taken back Suleimaniyah by the end of October, but American attempts to build up a united opposition to Saddam had clearly suffered a serious blow. The two Kurdish parties were brought together again in Ankara in October 1996, and signed a number of declarations of good intent, but these were ineffective, and a cycle of armed clashes and tenuous ceasefires continued. Two more ineffective rounds of talks were held as part of the 'Ankara Process' in January and May 1997. However, by the latter month the Kurdish position was sufficiently weakened that Turkey was able to carry out another massive cross-border military operation known as 'Operation Hammer'. In this and in subsequent operations in the autumn of 1997, Turkish and KDP forces attacked the PUK as well as the PKK, marking their involvement in as well as exploitation of the intra-Kurdish civil war.[26]

In spite of the setbacks of 1996–7, in the autumn of 1998 the Clinton administration made a renewed attempt to bring the two Kurdish sides together. Whether this was connected with contemporary plans for a possible land invasion of Iraq by the US is unclear (pp. 92–3). Under an agreement reached in Washington in September 1998, Barzani and Talabani committed themselves to power-sharing within the Kurdish region, ultimately to be part of a federal Iraq, with a reconvening of a Kurdish Assembly and the possible establishment of a unified security force. From the Turkish viewpoint, the important point was that the KDP and PUK both undertook to prevent the PKK from establishing bases in any part of the region. This did not entirely satisfy the Turkish side however, and in November 1998 the leaders of the two organizations were brought together once more in Ankara. As a result, they confirmed their commitments on the PKK, and asserted that a federal state of Iraq would not mean any infringements of Iraq's territorial integrity – a crucial point for the Turks.[27]

Implications and Projections

The outcome of events in 1997–8 showed that Turkey's position in the long-running problem of Iraq, although far from ideal, was not disastrous either. Thanks to the fierce hostility between Barzani and Talabani, and their respective organizations, Turkey had been able to build up some influence and control in the region, primarily by forging an alliance with the KDP. Ideally, the US would probably have preferred Turkish forces to stay out of Iraqi territory. However, America's dependence on Turkish approval for the continuation of 'Provide Comfort' (alias 'Northern Watch') plus its broad need to maintain good relations with its only treaty ally in the Middle East, meant that it was prepared to turn a blind eye to the frequent Turkish military incursions into northern Iraq, and to persuade the Iraqi Kurds to abandon support for the PKK. As a result, by 1998 the PKK's ability to launch attacks into Turkey from Iraqi territory was severely restricted. In the broader sphere, Turkey had also been able to strengthen its links with Washington via the entente with Israel, and to avoid permanent damage to its relationship with the Western powers generally, even during the testing period of the 'Refahyol' government. On the debit side, Turkey had not been able to cope with all the problems thrown up by the 1991 war, on a stable and predictable basis. At home, the PKK had been gravely weakened, but no serious attempt had been made to address political aspects of the Kurdish problem. In spite of the partial lifting of the embargo on trade with Iraq at the end of 1996, mutual trade was still way below its potential, and subject to Saddam's erratic conflicts with the UN weapons inspectors. By the end of the decade, the 'Provide Comfort' operation, originally set up as a stopgap response to the refugee crisis of April 1991, had acquired a degree of permanence, but those who were entrusted with enforcing it were beginning to ask what long-run aims it was supposed to serve, and what their 'exit strategy' (if there was one) was supposed to be. Western policy had contained Iraq, but had not overcome the danger which Saddam Hussein still appeared to represent.

Notes

1. Thanks to the quirks of the electoral system, Anap won fewer seats than the DYP in 1995, although it had a slightly higher share of the vote (19.7 per cent to 19.2 per cent). To be strictly accurate, Ecevit's DSP had gained a toehold in the 1991–5 parliament, with seven seats, but had failed to play more than a minor role. All election data are from Ali Eşref Turan, *Türkiye'de Seçmen Davranışı: Öncekceki Kırılmalar ve 2002 Seçimi*, Istanbul: Bilgi Ünıversitesi Yayınları, 2004, pp. 141 and 148, citing the Turkish State Institute of Statistics (now the Turkish Statistical Institute).
2. *Refah Partisi* (Welfare Party) and *Doğru Yol Partisi* (True Path Party).

3. For a fuller account and analysis of these events, see Michael M. Gunter, 'The Silent Coup: The Secularist–Islamist Struggle in Turkey', *Journal of South Asian and Middle Eastern Studies*, vol. 21, no. 3, 1998. On the Welfare Party in general, see M. Hakan Yavuz, *Islamic Political Identity in Turkey*, Oxford: Oxford University Press, 2003, ch. 9.

4. Quoted, Robert Olson, 'The Kurdish Question and Turkey's Foreign Policy, 1991–1995: From the Gulf War to the Incursion into Iraq', *Journal of South Asian and Middle Eastern Studies*, vol. 19, no. 1, 1995, p. 27.

5. See Aylin Güney, 'The People's Democracy Party', in Barry Rubin and Metin Heper (eds), *Political Parties in Turkey*, London: Cass, 2002, pp. 124–5.

6. Philip Robins, *Suits and Uniforms: Turkish Foreign Policy Since the Cold War*, London: Hurst, 2003, p. 329.

7. Kemal Kirişçi, 'The Kurdish Question and Turkish Foreign Policy', in Lenore G. Martin and Dimitris Keridis (eds), *The Future of Turkish Foreign Policy*, Cambridge MA and London: MIT Press, 2004, p. 283.

8. Ibid. pp. 295–6 and 305: *Briefing* (Ankara: weekly) 22 Feb. 1999, pp. 20–1: *Milliyet*, 30 June 1999.

9. For varying estimates, see Olson, 'Kurdish Question', p. 24, and Kemal Kirişçi and Gareth Winrow, *The Kurdish Question and Turkey: An Example of Trans-state Ethnic Conflict*, London: Cass, 1997, pp. 130 and 132.

10. *Briefing*, 15 Mar. 1999, p. 17.

11. Ibid., 21 June 1999, p. 17. On the forced evacuations and village burnings, see Kirişçi and Winrow, *Kurdish Question*, pp. 130–1.

12. Kirişçi, 'Kurdish Question', p. 305.

13. Kirişçi, 'Turkey and the Kurdish Safe-Haven in Northern Iraq', *Journal of South Asian and Middle Eastern Studies*, vol. 19, no. 3, 1995, pp. 35–6.

14. Mahmut Balı Aykan, 'Turkey's Policy in Northern Iraq, 1991–95', *Middle Eastern Studies*, vol. 32, no. 4, 1996, pp. 351 and 355; Michael M. Gunter, *The Kurds and the Future of Turkey*, New York NY: St Martin's Press, 1997, pp. 98–9.

15. Ofra Bengio, *The Turkish–Israeli Relationship: Changing Ties of Middle Eastern Outsiders*, New York NY and Basingstoke: Palgrave Macmillan, 2004, pp. 94–124; Robins, *Suits and Uniforms*, pp. 244–69.

16. Robins, *Suits and Uniforms*, pp. 146–7, 156–9 and 262–4 and Philip Robins, 'Turkish Foreign Policy under Erbakan', *Survival*, vol. 39, Summer 1997, pp. 85–6 and 93–4; Bengio, *Turkish–Israeli Relationship*, p. 110; Kirişçi, 'Kurdish Question', p. 294.

17. Mahmut Balı Aykan, 'The Turkey–US–Israel Triangle: Continuity, Change and Implications for Turkey's Post-Cold War Middle East Policy', *Journal of South Asian and Middle Eastern Studies*, vol. 22, no. 4, 1999, p. 27.

18. Olson, 'Kurdish Question', pp. 13–14; Aykan, 'Turkey's Policy', p. 358.

19. İhsan Gürkan, 'Turkish–Iraqi Relations: The Cold War and its Aftermath', *Turkish Review of Middle East Studies* (Istanbul: annual), vol. 9, 1996–7, pp.

59–60 and 62.

20. Although it was widely reported that this restriction was not strictly observed: Olson, 'Kurdish Question', pp. 14–15.

21. Gürkan, 'Turkish–Iraqi Relations', pp. 68–9.

22. Robins, *Suits and Uniforms*, pp. 330, 333 and 341; Charles Tripp, *A History of Iraq*, Cambridge: Cambridge University Press, 2000, p. 272; Kirişçi, 'Turkey and the Kurdish Safe-Haven', p. 37; Olson, 'Kurdish Question', pp. 18–19.

23. Olson, *Kurdish Question*, pp. 20–1; Gunter, *The Kurds and the Future*, pp. 120–1; Robins, *Suits and Uniforms*, p. 335.

24. Bill Park, *Turkey's Policy towards Northern Iraq: Problems and Perspectives*, London: Routledge, for International Institute for Strategic Studies, Adelphi Paper 374, 2005, p. 37; International Crisis Group, *Iraq: Allaying Turkey's Fears over Kurdish Ambitions*, Brussels: International Crisis Group, Middle East Report No. 35, 26 Jan. 2005, pp. 4–5 and 10–11.

25. Robins, *Suits and Uniforms*, p. 336; Aykan, 'Turkey's Policy', p. 357.

26. Tripp, *History of Iraq*, p. 273; Michael M. Gunter, 'The Foreign Policy of the Iraqi Kurds', *Journal of South Asian and Middle Eastern Studies*, vol. 20, no. 3, 1997, pp. 14–19; Robins, *Suits and Uniforms*, pp. 337–41.

27. Tripp, *History of Iraq*, p. 274; Kirişçi, 'Kurdish Question', pp. 307–8: details of the Washington and Ankara agreements from *Milliyet*, 2 Oct. and 9 Nov. 1998.

FOUR

Turkey, the US and the Second Gulf War, 1998–2003

The Gulf crisis of 1990–1 had left Turkey faced with complex problems, and substantially altered the parameters of its relationship with Iraq. However, its links with the United States remained generally stable and positive: while there were frictions with Washington over the 'Provide Comfort' operation, these were generally overcome. The second crisis of 2002–3 had many similarities within that of 1990–1, in that it also produced a war by the US against Iraq, and raised basic questions about what part Turkey could or should play in defeating Saddam Hussein. The outcome, however, was entirely different, so that for Turkey the second crisis was far from a repeat performance of the first.

In 1990–1 Turgut Özal had been able to play a positive role in ejecting Iraqi forces from Kuwait, and had left President George Bush highly appreciative of his efforts (p. 48). In contrast, the US invasion of Iraq launched by his son President George W. Bush in March 2003 produced the most serious collision between Ankara and Washington since the late 1970s, when the US Congress had imposed a temporary arms embargo on Turkey following the Turkish invasion of Cyprus in 1974, and proved much more difficult to resolve.[1] In the view of Mark Parris, a former US Ambassador to Ankara, Turkish policy during the Gulf crisis of 2003 was 'an unmitigated disaster for US–Turkish relations'.[2] Other American commentators, identified as being in the neo-conservative camp, such as Daniel Pipes, went even further, by suggesting in May 2005 that 'if things go as they have the past few years I expect Turkey before long to be more in the "foe" category, along with Saudi Arabia [*sic*], than the "friend" one'.[3] In similar vein, Michael Rubin concluded that 'the special relationship with Turkey is over ... Ankara is becoming more isolated than it has ever been before'.[4]

It can well be argued that these conclusions were much too gloomy, that they were far from universally supported, and were not well founded. Nevertheless, it was clear that US–Turkish relations had gone through a severe shock, which largely derived from the US-led invasion of Iraq. To narrate this story this chapter starts by looking at the domestic environment of Turkish politics between 1999 and 2002, and the main events in Turkish–US relations during these years. The focus then shifts to the emerging crisis over Iraq, and Turkish reactions to it. The advent of a new government in Ankara, under the Justice and Development Party in November 2002, and its handling of the Iraq crisis until the outbreak of war in March 2003, is then described. In Chapter 5, the narrative is concluded by outlining Turkish policies towards the US and Iraq in the aftermath of the war, up to the end of 2005, with an analysis of the story left to the final chapter.

The Domestic Political Background, 1999–2003

As in previous years, Turkey's foreign relations at the turn of the millennium were affected by its unstable domestic politics. The coalition government under Mesut Yılmaz which took office after the fall of the 'Refahyol' administration in June 1997 was hamstrung by the fact that it did not have a parliamentary majority, and was dependent on the outside support of the Republican People's Party (CHP) under Deniz Baykal (p. 68). In an attempt to resolve this dilemma, in July 1998 parliament voted to hold early elections in April 1999.[5] As Mesut Yılmaz came under increasing fire following allegations of serious corruption in his government, Baykal withdrew his support, and the coalition was defeated in a vote of confidence on 25 November 1998. After several weeks of uncertainty, on 17 January 1999 the Democratic Left Party (DSP) under Bülent Ecevit, the veteran leader of the centre left, established a minority caretaker administration, pending the elections. Ecevit then won an unexpected bonus when Abdullah Öcalan was brought back to Turkey, following his dramatic abduction in Nairobi on 16 February 1999 (p. 69). As the Prime Minister of the time, Ecevit won popular plaudits from a resurgent wave of nationalism. The other significant gainer was the Nationalist Action Party (MHP) under Devlet Bahçeli, which had persistently taken an ultra-hawkish line on the Kurdish question. As a result, when polling day arrived on 18 April 1999, the DSP emerged as the biggest party, with 22 per cent of the vote and 136 seats in the new parliament. The surprise winner was the MHP, which scored

18 per cent and won 129 seats. In spite of the wide ideological gap between the two parties, and deep suspicions of the MHP on the part of many members of the DSP (notably Ecevit's wife Rahşan)[6] the two parties formed a coalition government under Ecevit's premiership, on 28 May 1999. The Motherland Party, which had limped home with just 13 per cent of the poll and 86 seats, became the third partner in the coalition.

Although the new government did not present a convincing picture of solidarity, it was initially given the benefit of the doubt. In foreign policy, Ecevit's government started off well, beginning a political dialogue with Greece at the end of June 1999 which eventually blossomed into an unexpected rapprochement between the two countries.[7] However, its public standing was shattered by the massive earthquake which hit the industrial area round the Gulf of İzmit, near Istanbul, on 17 August 1999, in which over 17,000 people lost their lives, with around 25,000 injured and 250,000 left homeless. For the government, the political shock was equally devastating, since state agencies, notably the army and the quasi-governmental Red Crescent organization, were quite unprepared for the disaster. In contrast, voluntary groups and rescue teams from all over the world (including Greece) distinguished themselves with their promptness and efficiency.[8]

In December 1999 the government's fortunes took a turn for the better when, after years of dithering, the leaders of the European Union, meeting in Helsinki as the European Council, finally decided that Turkey could be a candidate for eventual accession to the EU, provided it met the 'Copenhagen criteria' of democratic norms as a preliminary condition. In the medium term, this was to have profound political effects in Turkey, by vastly improving the human rights regime, effectively shifting a large measure of power from the state to civil society, and forcing future governments into radical revisions of policies towards the internal Kurdish question. For the time being, however, the government was slow to act on this, failing to take any effective measures of liberalization until 2001.[9]

Meanwhile, its chronic failures in handling the economy destroyed the government's popularity. In an effort to reduce inflation (by then running at 70 per cent per annum) and stabilise the external value of the Turkish Lira, it negotiated a stand-by loan from the International Monetary Fund (IMF) of US$4 billion in December 1999, following this up with a 'supplemental reserve facility' from the fund for another $7.5 billion one year later. However, on 19 February 2001 this fragile recovery was shattered, when an open row erupted between Ecevit and Ahmet Necdet Sezer, a former Chief Justice of the Constitutional Court, who had succeeded Demirel as President of the Republic after the latter retired in May 2000. President Sezer accused the Prime Minister of having failed to investigate reports of widespread malpractice in three state banks, or dismiss the Minister of Energy, who was also accused of corrupt practices. Ecevit refused to accept these accusations, and instead angrily criticized the President for 'inappropriate' behaviour.[10] As a result, Turkey's nervous financial markets crashed. The Turkish Lira lost half its value in two months, and the cost of bailing out the failed banks increased the government debt to about 100 per cent of GDP. Kemal Derviş, a former Vice-President of the World Bank, was brought back to Ankara to join the cabinet, and head a rescue operation, with aid from the IMF. In achieving this, he received crucial help from the US government, which was apparently anxious to prop up an important ally.[11] Meanwhile, however, the economy was pushed into sharp recession, with a fall in GDP of just under 9 per cent for 2001.[12] Thanks to IMF backing, which came with tight strings attached, the economy began to recover in 2002, but by then the political damage had been done, as the ruling parties lost virtually all the public support they had garnered in 1999.

By the spring and summer of 2002 the Ecevit government was clearly falling apart. The Prime Minister's health (he was by now 77 years old) had been failing for some time. In May 2002 he was hospitalized twice with a variety of maladies, and unable to carry out his normal duties for around two months.[13] In July 2002 his successful Foreign Minister, İsmail Cem, resigned to form his own New Turkey Party (YTP) where he was joined by fifty-eight ex-DSP backbenchers, robbing the government of its majority. The leader of the MHP, Devlet Bahçeli, who had been in sharp conflict with the rest of the government over human rights reforms demanded by the EU, then sprang a surprise on his coalition partners by demanding early general elections, which he mistakenly believed he could win. On 31 July 2002 parliament voted to hold general elections on 3 November by a majority of 440 votes to 62, the only dissenters apparently being from Ecevit's DSP.[14]

As the election campaign gathered pace in the autumn of 2002 it became clear that the initiative was passing into the hands of a new actor on the national political scene. A member of Necmettin Erbakan's Welfare Party since his student days, Recep Tayyip Erdoğan had been a successful mayor of Istanbul between 1994 and 1998, when he was convicted of 'stirring up hatred and enmity with regard to ... religion'[15] and sentenced to ten months in prison as well as a lifetime ban from participation in politics. Following the closure of the Welfare Party in January 1998 (p. 68), Erdoğan emerged as the leader of a group within its successor, the Virtue Party (*Fazilet Partisi*, or FP), known as the 'renewalists'. This opposed Erbakan, and sought to convert the party to a modernist, pro-Western, liberal-conservative stance, with tinges of Islamism. After an unsuccessful attempt by the 'renewalists' to take over the leadership of the Virtue Party at its first national convention in May 2000, and the enforced closure of the party in June 2001, Necmettin Erbakan set up a Felicity Party (*Saadet Partisi*, or SP) nominally under his lieutenant and proxy Recai Kutan. However, this failed to capture more than a tiny fraction of public support. Meanwhile, Erdoğan and his supporters set up the Justice and Development Party (AKP) on 14 August 2001.[16] The new party abandoned Erbakan's former call for an Islamic order, and strongly backed the improvement of human rights and Turkey's bid to join the EU. In the run-up to the elections, the AKP had a clear lead in the opinion polls, as millions of voters deserted the government parties, opting for the AKP as the best alternative which had a good chance of winning. More positively, Erdoğan, who was an appealing public orator, captured the support of most of those who had previously voted for the Welfare Party and its successors, as well as much of the liberal centre-right. As the election results came in, it was clear that the AKP had won by a landslide. None of the previous ruling parties passed the 10 per cent threshold which they would have needed to win any seats in parliament. With around 46 per cent of the vote going to parties scoring less than 10 per cent (and thus effectively discounted) the AKP won 363 of the 550 seats on 34.3 per cent of the poll. As the only other party to pass the 10 per cent threshold, the nominally centre-left Republican People's Party (CHP) came in a poor second, with 19.4 per cent of the poll and 178 seats.

The AKP's election victory gave Turkey a single-party government with a solid majority for the first time since 1991. However, the continuing ban on participation in politics imposed on Erdoğan in 1998 had the absurd result that the leader of the winning party could not even become a member of parliament, let alone Prime Minister. Accordingly, his principal lieutenant, Abdullah Gül, took over as temporary premier on 16 November 2002. The problem was partly resolved on 11 December, when parliament passed a motion altering Article 86 of the constitution, by deleting the provision that those convicted for 'ideological and anarchic activities' (which included Erdoğan's alleged offence of 1998) would be debarred from running as parliamentary candidates.[17] Meanwhile, the High Electoral Commission, as the judicial body which oversees elections in Turkey, ordered a re-run of the election in the south-eastern province of Siirt, due to serious irregularities in the November poll.[18] This allowed Erdoğan to compete successfully in a by-election in Siirt on 9 March 2003, and to take over as Prime Minister on 12 March, with Abdullah Gül as his Foreign Minister.[19]

Turkey, the US and Iraq, 1998–2002: The Emerging Conflict

For all the upsets in domestic politics, and continuing uncertainties in its relations with Brussels as well as the internal Kurdish problem, Turkey's relationship with the United States during the late 1990s could be seen in retrospect as something of a honeymoon period. In Washington, the Clinton administration strongly supported

Turkey's bid to join the EU, and evidently valued its actual or potential role in the Middle East, the Balkans and Transcaucasia. For the Turks, the US government's role in securing the arrest of Abdullah Öcalan was another feather in its cap. The strength of the alliance was put under the spotlight in November 1999, when President Clinton and other world leaders visited Istanbul for a summit meeting of the Organization for Security and Cooperation in Europe (OSCE). The President stayed on in Turkey for several days after the summit, being accorded the rare privilege of addressing the Turkish parliament. In his address, and a subsequent press conference, he stressed his appreciation of Turkey's role as a NATO ally, and claimed that a democratic Turkey would be a key to the shaping of the next century. The Turkish–US relationship was now described as one of 'strategic partnership'. With his wife and daughter, Bill Clinton visited the victims of the İzmit earthquake in their tents, showing striking informality and sympathy, which was starkly contrasted with the usually aloof and dour demeanour of most of Turkey's own politicians. In particular, a photograph of the President holding a baby who had survived the disaster conveyed a heart-warming image, which many Turks remember long after the event.[20] The President's message may have been long on rhetoric and short on specifics – it was hard to say, for instance, what the 'strategic partnership' was supposed to amount to now that the cold war was over – but his visit certainly appeared to mark a high-water mark in the alliance.

The installation of George W. Bush as President in January 2001 does not seem to have disturbed this relationship, even though the new administration initially seemed to be giving a lower priority to its relations with Turkey, and policy towards the Middle East in general, than Bill Clinton had done. The horrific terrorist attacks in New York and Washington of 11 September 2001 dramatically changed the President's priorities, but the immediate effect was to enhance rather than damage the 'strategic partnership' – indeed it gave it more relevance and urgency. The Ecevit government and the Turkish parliament had no difficulty in supporting the President's global campaign against terrorism, and the subsequent attack on the Taliban regime in Afghanistan, since they could convincingly argue that they had more experience of dealing with a terrorist threat than the US, or most of their European allies. Immediately after the tragedy of 9/11, President Sezer sent a fulsome message of sympathy to President Bush. Bülent Ecevit repeated this message, adding that 'the Turkish government is as ready as ever to cooperate with you'.[21] All parties in Turkey, including the pro-Islamist Felicity Party and the newly founded AKP, added their voices to the chorus of support. The Taliban had virtually no supporters in Turkey. Hence, on 10 October 2001 the Turkish parliament easily passed a resolution (in Turkish, *tezkere*) authorizing the despatch of troops to support coalition troops in Afghanistan, in accordance with Article 92 of the constitution (see p. 41).[22] Following a suggestion from US Secretary of State Colin Powell, who visited Ankara on 5 December 2001, Turkey took over command of the International Security Assistance Force (ISAF) in Kabul in June 2002 for a six-month period, with a detachment of 1,400 soldiers.[23] At this stage, as Mark Parris had remarked at the end of 2001, 'Turkey's response to 11 September has been everything one would expect of a "strategic partner".'[24] A visiting Republican congressman, Curt Weldon, even described Turkey as a 'shining crown jewel'.[25]

Nonetheless, a dark cloud was looming on the horizon, as the administration began to seriously consider an armed intervention against Iraq, identified by George W. Bush, in his State of the Union address to Congress in January 2002, as part of an 'axis of evil' allegedly giving global support to terrorism. Turkey had no difficulty in supporting US policy in Afghanistan – a faraway country in which it had virtually no material interests – but a US invasion of neighbouring Iraq threatened far more serious consequences for Ankara, re-awakening all the worries which had surfaced during the Gulf crisis of 1990–1.

In fact, 'regime change' in Iraq – originally expected to be effected by an internal rebellion or palace coup – had become the policy of the American government in 1995 (p. 76). This was confirmed in 1998 when the US Senate unanimously passed the Iraq Liberation Act, voting to give US$97 million to the Iraqi opposition. Additionally, and although it was not public knowledge at the time, it appears that President Bush and his colleagues were not the initiators of the plan for a land invasion or Iraq by US forces, but that it had first come onto the Turkish–US agenda in November 1998. On 31 October 1998 the United Nations efforts to force Iraq to remove weapons of mass destruction appeared to have reached breakdown, as Saddam Hussein unilaterally announced that all activities by UN weapons inspectors (UNSCOM) would cease. The US government decided that tougher measures would have to be taken, since Saddam's action followed a long series of flagrant violations of UN resolutions by Iraq. On 6 November 1998 President Clinton's Secretary of Defense, William Cohen, visited Ankara as part of a tour taking in Britain, Egypt, Saudi Arabia, Kuwait and Jordan, and had discussions with the Turkish Defence Minister İsmet Sezgin and President Demirel. Without giving away any details, Cohen stated that 'we will ask our friends for help in a possible military operation' while Sezgin said that Cohen had 'presented his thoughts to us and Mr Demirel'.[26] However, it appears that in his meeting with Demirel, Cohen had produced a letter from President Clinton to 'Dear Suleyman', stating that if Saddam Hussein continued to defy the UN, then a regime change in Iraq by military means including 'the introduction of ground forces' could come onto the agenda. General Anthony Zinni, the Central Forces (CENTCOM) commander, who was responsible for US forces in the Gulf and accompanied Cohen, added that the US expected Turkey's active participation in such an operation.

Demirel's response was that the idea would be mistaken and risky. He accepted that Saddam was a threat to the region and to Turkey, but suggested that, rather than invade Iraq, the US should identify a rival to Saddam, and overthrow the Iraqi dictator by organizing a palace coup. The American visitors were evidently unimpressed by this, since a previous coup attempt in 1996 had failed dismally.[27] The immediate US reaction was thus confined to 'Operation Desert Fox' in which British and US planes used the İncirlik air base for massive strikes against Iraq, launched on 17 December 1998. Secretary of State Madeleine Albright informed Demirel of the operation shortly before it started, although there were some doubts in Ankara about whether it could actually be fitted in to the remit of 'Northern Watch'.[28]

In spite of this initial resistance, and although it did not have support on this from any of its allies except Britain, it appears that the Clinton administration did not abandon the idea of a major military operation against Iraq. It continued to consider the idea after the installation of the Ecevit government in April 1999, although it suspected that Ecevit was basically a 'third-worldist' and knew that he was unlikely to support it. Nonetheless, Clinton returned to the charge in November 1999. During his visit to Ankara after the OSCE summit he reportedly told Demirel that action against Saddam would not be immediate, but that the US wanted Turkey to be on its side when it happened. Demirel was anxious to strengthen Turkey's relations with the West, but was constrained by the fact that he knew he would have to retire from the presidency in May 2000.[29] Timing was also an important consideration on the US side. The Pentagon considered that any invasion of Iraq would have to take place during the winter, to be completed by the spring, so as to avoid the burning heat of Iraq during the summer. However, presidential elections were due to be held in November 2000, with the installation of a new President in the following January. It would not be possible to launch a war against Iraq in such conditions. Accordingly, the issue remained unsettled when Bill Clinton left office in January 2001.[30]

Within the new Republican administration, the idea of taking tough action against Iraq did not entirely derive from the after-shock of 11 September 2001, since conservatives in Congress as well as the incoming Secretary of Defense Donald Rumsfeld had for some time supported the idea of an aggressive policy against Saddam.[31] What seems to have been changed by 9/11 was the commitment of President Bush to this proposal. The plan was strongly supported by Rumsfeld and the ideologues of neo-conservatism like Deputy Defense Secretary Paul Wolfowitz, and the Under-Secretary of Defense for Policy, Douglas Feith. Against this, Secretary of State Colin Powell and Rich Armitage, his deputy in the State Department, were far more cautious and sceptical about belligerent notions of dealing with Saddam, besides being bitterly critical of the neo-conservatives in the Department of Defense.[32] After leaving office in 2005, Powell was to complain that he had often been cut out of the decision-making loop in Washington.[33] In Ankara, Bülent Ecevit was highly unenthusiastic about the prospect of a war with Iraq, just as he had been when it had been suggested by the Clinton administration. As he told a television interviewer on 21 September 2001 'it would be extremely inappropriate to spread out the targets' in the battle against terrorism.[34] This was the first of several warnings issued by Ecevit, to the effect that an invasion of Iraq could result in the partition of the country, and the de-stabilization of the entire region.[35] Other Turkish reactions were that Turkey might support the US, provided a link could be proved between Iraq and the terrorist assaults, and/or action against Iraq had the backing of the UN Security Council.[36] Since neither of these conditions were fulfilled, Turkey's position was left doubtful, to say the least.

The proposal was brought up again when Colin Powell visited Ankara on 5 December 2001. Asked about Iraq, the Secretary of State replied that 'we have asked for nothing from Turkey because no decisions or recommendations have been made to President Bush', although Ecevit was reported to have told Powell of the 'anxieties' Turkey felt about the idea.[37] In return, Ecevit paid his first visit to President Bush in Washington on 16 January 2002. After discussion of the Cyprus question, Vice President Dick Cheney told Ecevit that there were suspicions that Saddam had continued to procure weapons of mass destruction, and supported terrorist movements. When diplomatic channels were exhausted, which would not be long off, military action would be inevitable. Ecevit replied that Turkey did not support Saddam's regime, but wanted to preserve the territorial integrity of Iraq. The chief Turkish worry evidently was that if Saddam were overthrown, then Iraq would be partitioned, and the Iraqi Kurds would break away and take over control of the cities of Kirkuk and Mosul. The former, with its important oil reserves, could form the basis of an independent Kurdish state, with potentially disastrous effects on Turkey's hold over its own Kurdish minority. In effect, opposition to Kurdish independence, or even wide autonomy within a federal state, and to Kurdish control of Kirkuk, were two of Turkey's crucial 'red lines' in its approach to the future of Iraq.[38] This anxiety was sharpened by the fact that the Iraqi Kurdish leadership was meanwhile negotiating with the Pentagon, pressing for a Kurdish takeover of Kirkuk, and possibly Mosul, in return for help to an American operation against Saddam. Bush's response to Ecevit was that no immediate action against Iraq was planned, but that if it happened Turkey would be 'consulted' first and the territorial integrity of Iraq would be preserved, although it might be reconstructed as a federal state. Nor did Ecevit receive any assurances of US economic support to compensate Turkey for the effects of a war on Iraq.[39]

On 19–20 March 2002, Dick Cheney visited Ankara, as the last stop in a tour of Middle Eastern capitals which was evidently designed to test reactions to a possible invasion of Iraq. According to Ecevit, the Vice-President told him there would be no military operation against Iraq in the 'near future', but if there were there would be an 'understanding' attitude by Washington towards Turkey's economic concerns.[40] It thus appears that the Bush administration was seriously considering an attack on Iraq. It was clearly aware of Ecevit's misgivings, however, and at this stage it does not seem to have envisaged an active Turkish role in the operation. Meanwhile, Ecevit's reaction was to try to head off the danger of a US attack on Iraq by persuading Saddam Hussein to allow the UN to re-start the weapons inspection programme. On 1 February 2002 he wrote to Saddam to this effect, but received a blunt rejection from Baghdad.[41]

As these uncertainties continued during the summer of 2002, it also appeared that if Saddam were overthrown, then Turkey could face a head-on collision with the Iraqi Kurds. In early August the Turkish Minister of Defence, Sabahattin Çakmakoğlu, who was a member of the Nationalist Action Party, made some singularly ill-advised remarks suggesting that Turkey had not abandoned its old claim to Mosul. This did not reflect official Turkish policy, but provoked a predictable reaction from Massoud Barzani, who told the German weekly *Die Zeit* that if Turkey intervened in northern Iraq it would become 'the graveyard of the Turkish army'. Barzani added that although an independent Kurdistan was his greatest desire, he recognized that for the time being the Kurds would have to be content with autonomy within Iraq. Kirkuk, meanwhile, would 'remain the heart of Kurdistan'.[42] Needless to say, Barzani's remarks provoked a hostile reaction in the Turkish press, with speculation that if the Kurds declared their independence in a post-Saddam Iraq, or took over Kirkuk, then Turkey might invade from the north.[43] Meanwhile, there were reports that, as a last resort, the Iraqi Kurds might even be prepared to cut a deal with Saddam Hussein to keep the Turkish army out of their country.[44]

In spite of all these warning signals – plus the fact that the Ecevit government was clearly on its last legs and in no position to take any important initiatives – the US military planners continued to pursue the idea of an attack on Iraq, and appear to have assumed that they could get Turkish support for it. In mid-June 2002 the Turkish embassy in Washington reported to Ankara that the US would definitely attack Iraq, with or without UN approval. It would like to have Turkish cooperation, but the lack of it would not prevent an invasion. This became clearer on 14–17 July, when Paul Wolfowitz visited Turkey and had discussions with Şükrü Sina Gürel, who had recently succeeded İsmail Cem as Ecevit's Foreign Minister, as well as representatives of other political parties, including Abdullah Gül. Reportedly, Wolfowitz had plans for the invasion of Iraq in his briefcase, and made it clear that the US was determined to intervene in Iraq, although no final decision had been made at this stage. In later discussions with the Turkish General Staff and Foreign Ministry, the Turkish side urged that if Saddam were overthrown, then the US should not allow a Kurdish state to be established in Iraq, and should take care of Turkey's economic risks. They concluded that the US military wanted to use Turkish territory for an invasion of Iraq since this would make its task easier. It was recognized that the Turkish government would probably change, but it was thought that the Turkish military chiefs could persuade a successor government to go along with the plan, given the traditionally close relationship between themselves and the US military. In return, Turkey would want the US to support its bid to start accession negotiations with the European Union, and on the Cyprus question.[45]

Fuller details of what the US intended came through Uğur Ziyal, Under-Secretary at the Turkish Foreign Ministry, who was in Washington on 26 August 2002 and had a discussion with Donald Rumsfeld via a video-link (Rumsfeld was out of town at the time).

Although no definite decision to invade Iraq had been taken at this stage, the Secretary for Defense told Ziyal that, as part of the invasion plan, the US intended to put 75,000–80,000 troops into northern Iraq, via Turkish territory. Preparations would have to start several months before, so as to improve airfields, ports, roads, and railways in Turkey between the Mediterranean and the Iraqi frontier. At the end of September General Charles Wald, deputy commander of US forces in Europe, filled in the details, confirming that if the plan went ahead 80,000 troops would be deployed via Turkey together with 250 aircraft, which would have the use not just of İncirlik, but also of eleven other air bases in Turkey.[46] Apparently, these proposals came as a shock to the Turkish side, which had hitherto assumed that the US would only want the use of Turkish airfields and the passage of relatively small special forces across Turkish territory. In Turkish eyes, America seemed to be demanding a blank cheque. In a memorandum drawn up on 15 October, the Foreign Ministry pointed out that such an operation would be unprecedented in the history of the Turkish Republic, and that it would be strongly opposed by public opinion, arguing that it could only be carried through with backing from the United Nations. Bülent Ecevit evidently agreed with this assessment; when he handed over the premiership on 19 November his last advice to Abdullah Gül was reportedly not to get involved in Iraq.[47]

The American military did not originally propose that Turkey should itself put any forces into Iraq, but this suggestion came from the Turkish side, originally as part of a plan to set up a series of refugee camps in northern Iraq and the border region of Turkey. This was the part of the plan about which the Americans were least enthusiastic, and they only accepted it reluctantly. While the

Turks had other motives as well – notably the perceived need to have some military presence in northern Iraq so as to deter the Kurds from declaring independence, and perhaps exercise some leverage over the US itself – there was genuine anxiety in Ankara to avoid a repeat of the refugee crisis of April 1991. With the same objectives in mind, during October 2002 the Turkish army began a build-up of its forces on the Iraqi border, reaching a total of 50,000 by December.[48] According to one account, at a meeting at the presidential mansion on 5 October, President Sezer, Prime Minister Ecevit, Foreign Minister Gürel, and the Chief of the Turkish General Staff, General Hilmi Özkök, agreed to send a Turkish Army Corps into Iraq without waiting for the Americans, but it was then decided to abandon this idea thanks to the pending elections.[49] Turkish policy had also muddied the waters by boosting the claims of the Iraqi Turcoman Front (p. 76) to a share of power in a post-Saddam Iraq. The ITF urged that if the Kurds were to have a self-governing entity in the north of the country, then the Turcomans should have one too, based on Kirkuk, which they regarded as their ancestral home. Under Turkish pressure, and in the face of opposition by the KDP, the ITF was belatedly incorporated into the US-sponsored Iraqi opposition in the autumn of 2002.[50]

Meanwhile, Ecevit, Sezer, and General Özkök also agreed that any joint action would depend on a decision by the United Nations. This was put into question on 11 October, when the US Congress passed a resolution allowing the administration to start military action against Iraq without waiting for authorization from the UN. Nevertheless, President Sezer continued to insist on this condition when President Bush telephoned him on 24 October. Meanwhile, on 21–22 October Generals Tommy Franks and Joseph Ralston, respectively commanders of US forces in the Gulf (CENTCOM) and Europe visited Ankara for talks with General Özkök. The latter is reported to have reminded his visitors that the Turkish army could not promise anything by itself, since carrying through the plan would depend on authorization by the Turkish parliament, under Article 92 of the constitution. Any decision would have to be postponed until after the elections.[51] The authorities in Ankara thus had a fairly good idea of what the US intended, but crucial questions remained unanswered when Turkey went to the polls on 3 November 2002. On the US side, the perceived need to reach an agreement with Turkey meant that the planned date for an invasion, originally fixed for January 2003, had to be postponed until the second half of March.[52]

In the Eye of the Storm: November 2002–March 2003

Although serious tension in relations between Turkey and the US over Iraq seemed quite likely by the autumn of 2002, a striking feature of the Turkish election campaign of October–November was that it gave almost no attention to it. The main Turkish parties seemed to shy off making any commitments on this score. With opinion polls showing it clearly in the lead, and thus likely to form the next government, the AKP's election manifesto restricted itself to calling for the preservation of the territorial integrity of Iraq, and full implementation of UN decisions on disarmament by the Iraqi government.[53] This indecision may be blamed for the subsequent crisis in Turkish–US relations, but at the time it seemed hard to avoid. The specific proposals which the US was putting to Turkey were not public knowledge at the time, nor had President Bush taken a definite decision to invade Iraq, so it was hard for the parties to announce what position they would take. Initially, it appears that Tayyip Erdoğan and Abdullah Gül, like Bülent Ecevit, were far from supportive of the US plan, and seem to have assumed that Turkey could only cooperate if the action were endorsed by the UN Security Council, which remained uncertain. On 8 November 2002 the Security Council issued its Resolution 1441, offering Iraq 'a final opportunity to comply with its disarmament obligations' and threatening 'serious consequences' if its conditions were not met. However, it did not specifically authorize the use of force if Iraq failed to comply.[54] To add to the uncertainty, until mid-December 2002, Turkish attentions were focused on the EU, rather than Iraq, since the European Council was due to meet on 12–13 December to decide whether to start accession negotiations with Turkey. In the event, the Turks received a reasonably encouraging decision from the EU,[55] but by then valuable time had been lost in dealing with the problem of Iraq.

In spite of this, the Pentagon seems to have assumed that the establishment of the AKP government had increased the prospects of securing an agreement with Turkey. On 3 December Paul Wolfowitz returned to Ankara, with further details of the American plan. An outline of these was published in the press on 13 December, so that they became publicly known for the first time.[56] In discussions with Abdullah Gül, Wolfowitz outlined a three-stage process in which the US military would first inspect bases, ports, and communications in Turkey, to be followed by a 'site preparation stage' in which these would be improved to meet the needs of the US forces. The third stage would consist of the stationing of air and land forces (now fixed as 60,000 troops). Wolfowitz announced after his visit that 'Turkish support is assured', but in fact the government was still circumspect, and refused to give the US definite access to Turkish territory.[57] Gül agreed to implement the first stage, without committing Turkey to the second two, and the government gave permission for this on 18 December 2002.[58]

Although he was not yet Prime Minister, but officially only the chairman of the ruling party, Tayyip Erdoğan was received by President Bush for the first time in the White House on 10 December 2002. The Turkish press put a positive gloss on the meeting, and the American side gained the impression that Erdoğan would give full support to the US strategy.[59] However, he later denied that he had given any specific undertakings to the President, saying merely that it would be important to persuade other Muslim countries to join the coalition. Erdoğan's caution reflected serious opposition to the US plan by many members of his own party, including Deputy Premier Ertuğrul Yalçınbayır, the speaker of parliament, Bülent Arınç, and all the members of the party's subcommittees on human rights and foreign relations.[60] Inevitably, backbench MPs were influenced by public opinion polls taken in December 2002 showing that over 85 per cent of the public were opposed to the expected action against Iraq, rising to 94 per cent in January 2003.[61]

Meanwhile, Turkey's military commanders were laying out the options to the government. At a meeting with Gül on 23 December 2002 the General Staff listed the possibilities. Its conclusion was that, even though this would be highly unwelcome, the US would invade Iraq anyway, so Turkey should not stand aside. The number of US troops allowed to enter Turkey should be reduced from the 80,000 proposed by the Pentagon. Gül's reaction is reported to have been that he could never explain this to his own party.[62] Nonetheless, the Turkish military chiefs continued to press the plan, including the proposal that Turkish troops should occupy a 'security belt' stretching 30–40 km into Iraq as part of the operation – a project which the US side had not so far agreed to.[63] The idea reflected the proposal which Turgut Özal had put forward in April 1991 to establish a limited 'security zone' just south of the Turkey–Iraq border, to shelter Kurdish refugees (p. 49). This set the tone for the subsequent debate. In Turkey, unlike Britain, the main part of the argument was not about whether Saddam Hussein still had weapons of mass destruction or was a security threat to his neighbours, but whether it would be good policy to support the United States, which now seemed to be determined to invade Iraq, with or without Turkey or a follow-up to Resolution 1441 from the UN.

During January 2003 a major part of Turkey's diplomatic effort was devoted to an attempt to head off war with Iraq by building up a coalition of Middle Eastern nations to put pressure on Saddam Hussein, and by direct contacts with the Iraqi government. The difficulty it faced was that, although none of the Middle Eastern governments which Turkey approached supported Saddam, none of them wanted Iraq to be occupied by the US, and none were prepared to take separate military action. On 24 January Turkey hosted a meeting in Istanbul with the foreign ministers of Jordan, Syria, Saudi Arabia, Iran and Egypt. This called on the Iraqi government to 'move irreversibly and sincerely towards assuming their responsibilities in restoring peace and stability in the region', and insisted on retaining the territorial integrity of Iraq.[64] The last commitment was of value to Turkey, since it confirmed that none of its neighbours supported the establishment of an independent Kurdish state, but the main objective, of preventing a war, remained unachieved.

Meanwhile, the government continued its efforts to persuade Saddam to back down, although Gül was told by the Egyptian President Hosni Mubarak that this effort would be hopeless, and Bülent Ecevit had engaged in a fruitless meeting with the then Iraqi Foreign Minister Tariq Aziz in October 2002. On 11 January Gül sent the Iraqi dictator a letter telling him this was his last opportunity to avoid war, and that he should fully comply with UN resolutions. The letter was taken to Baghdad by Minister of State Kürşad Tüzmen, nominally at the head of a trade delegation, since this was believed to be the only way of making sure that Saddam read it. Saddam's response was that Turkey should instead persuade the US not to invade his country. Later, on 3 February, Saddam's deputy Taha Yassin Ramadan and his new Foreign Minister Naji Sabri visited Ankara for secret talks with Gül, Foreign Minister Yaşar Yakış, and Uğur Ziyal, but this again failed to produce any concessions from the Iraqi side. It was later reported that Gül had even offered Saddam a guarantee of his personal safety if he stepped down, either in Turkey or another country, and that the US government knew of it at the time.[65]

At this stage, Turkey's military chiefs were still unenthusiastic about the American plan. In early January, for instance, General Özkök admitted that a war against Iraq 'would be against Turkey's interests ... I have not heard anyone here say "let there be a war"'.[66] This reflected remarks by Abdullah Gül, who told the Turkish parliament that Turkey 'could not afford to be seen as a country encouraging war'.[67] Nonetheless, on 31 January 2003, the National

Security Council in Ankara took a crucial step on the path to military action by agreeing that, although Turkey was in favour of a peaceful resolution to the Iraq crisis, and that 'a military option would undoubtedly have regrettable effects from the point of view of regional countries', the government was recommended to lay before parliament a resolution allowing the 'military measures deemed necessary to protect Turkey's national interests'. It added that 'international legitimacy' would be one of the 'basic principles directing Turkey's attitude', without saying specifically that this would mean passage of another resolution by the UN Security Council.[68]

In effect, it appeared that by this stage the AKP leaders as well as the generals had come round to the view that, like it or not, Turkey would do best to play its part in the US plan. Their difficulty was that they could not be sure that they could persuade their own party to support it in parliament. On 5 February Tayyip Erdoğan told the AKP's parliamentary group that Turkey could not afford to stay out of the expected military operation if it were to have any influence over subsequent events, much as Turgut Özal had in September 1990 (p. 39).[69] On the following day the government laid a resolution before parliament authorizing the second stage of the three-stage process, authorizing US military personnel to upgrade Turkish ports, air bases and transport links in the south-east of the country, without definitely committing Turkey to support the expected US attack on Iraq. In the vote, the resolution won the support of 318 of the 517 deputies present in the house, with 193 opposing and 16 abstentions.[70] The ballot confirmed that there was much reluctance within the ruling party to support the American plan. Unfortunately, this fact was not effectively conveyed to the US government.

Following the passage of the resolution, US military personnel and equipment began landing in Turkey on 12 February, to complete the communications upgrade.[71] Meanwhile, to meet the danger that Iraq might mount a pre-emptive strike, the government applied to NATO for defensive support under the North Atlantic Treaty. This included the supply of Patriot air defence missiles, AWACS surveillance aircraft, and drugs and experts to counter possible chemical and biological attacks. Initially, the request was blocked by France, Germany and Belgium, provoking sharp criticism of the 'old Europe' by Donald Rumsfeld and President Bush. However, on 16 February, Lord Robertson, the Secretary-General of NATO, was able to circumvent this obstacle by taking a decision at the NATO military council, on which France is not represented. The German and Belgian governments dropped their objections, and the aid to Turkey was approved and delivered.[72]

As negotiations between the Turkish and US authorities continued during February 2003, two factors delayed an agreement, and even appeared to put it in serious jeopardy. The first was Turkish demands for financial compensation to meet Turkey's expected losses, which had been part of the Turkish agenda since March 2002. This mainly derived from the popular perception in Turkey that it had never been adequately compensated for its economic losses following the 1991 war, and real fears that the Turkish economy was still barely out of the casualty ward, after the economic crash of 2001. On 13–14 February a delegation led by Yaşar Yakış and Ali Babacan, Minister of State with special responsibility for the economy, visited Washington for talks with Secretary of State Colin Powell, his political adviser Marc Grossman, and senior Treasury and economic officials. It was reported that the Turkish side asked for as much as US$92 billion in aid to compensate for Turkey's estimated losses during the five years following the expected war. The American response came nowhere near this: by 20 February the US was offering US$6 billion in grants and US$10 billion in loans, but this still fell short of what the Turks were pressing for, and the issue remained unresolved until the last minute.[73]

The prolonged haggling over money seriously delayed a decision by the Turkish parliament, much to the annoyance and expense of the US. On 4 February Gül had told Vice President Cheney that he would submit a draft resolution to parliament on the 18th of that month, and the Bush administration pressed for this date, but the arguments over money made it impossible to meet this deadline. Since parliament would then go on holiday for the Muslim Festival of the Sacrifice (*Kurban Bayramı*) it would not be possible to take a vote until 25 February at the earliest. By this stage, around three dozen ships with tanks and heavy equipment, plus almost 35,000 soldiers of the US army's Fourth Infantry Division had already arrived in the eastern Mediterranean and were waiting to unload in Turkish ports, at a cost of US$1.5 million per day.[74]

A second and more ominous threat to the invasion plan was fierce opposition by the Iraqi Kurds to the involvement of Turkish forces. The US side had evidently been aware of this problem from early on. At the end of his visit to Ankara in December 2002, Paul Wolfowitz showed some sensitivity to Turkish concerns by stating that none of the forces involved, including the Iraqi Kurds, should have sole control of Kirkuk, but that it would be wrong for Turkish forces to intervene unilaterally in northern Iraq, and that talks should be held between Turkey, the US and the Iraqi Kurdish leaders to coordinate policies and 'to reach an agreement on what are the red lines'.[75] However, no such agreement including the Iraqi Kurds was negotiated. Instead, in December 2002 the KDP and PUK adopted a joint platform calling for a Kurdish self-governing area within a loose Iraqi federation, in which the Kurds would have their own armed forces, with Kirkuk as their capital, and the constitutional right to secede from Iraq.[76] As Henry Kissinger put it, 'Kurds define self-government as only microscopically distinguishable from independence'[77] – the *bête noire* for Turkish policy makers.

On 24 February 2003 a spokesman for the KDP warned that the presence of Turkish troops in Kurdish territory could lead to 'uncontrolled exchanges of fire' with the *peshmerga* forces. On the following day the Kurdish parliament of northern Iraq unanimously passed a resolution rejecting the entry of 'foreign' forces (notably, Turkish ones) to the region. This was combined with massive anti-Turkish demonstrations in Iraqi Kurdistan.[78] Behind the scenes, on 1 February, a draft agreement had been reached between Turkey and the US on rules of engagement for the Turkish troops who were to occupy the 'security belt' along the Iraqi side of the Turkish–Iraqi border. However Zalmay Khalilzad, President Bush's Special Representative in the Middle East, then reported from Arbil that the Iraqi Kurdish leaders would oppose the entry of any Turkish troops into Iraq. On 4 February he visited Ankara and conveyed this information to Foreign Minister Yakış, who replied that this would make it difficult to reach an agreement.[79] Over two and a half years later, in December 2005, Khalilzad, who was by this time the US ambassador in Baghdad, admitted that he had 'made many efforts to prevent Turkey from entering Iraq'.[80] Nonetheless, the Pentagon either underrated the danger, or thought that the risk of a clash between the Turkish army and the Iraqi Kurds was worth taking, as part of the deal to allow US troops access to the 'northern front'.

To put the invasion plan into action, on 8 February the Pentagon had prepared a list of the forces it wished to enter Turkey.[81] This formed the basis of three more memoranda of understanding between the two governments which were not finalized until 1 March, the same day the crucial vote took place in parliament. These dealt with military, political and economic aspects respectively. On the military side, the maximum number of troops the US would be able to send to Turkey, or via Turkey to Iraq, would be reduced to 62,000. The US air force would deploy 255 war planes and sixty-five helicopters at Turkish air bases at İncirlik, Diyarbakır, and Batman. Turkey would be entitled to deploy up to 60,000 troops in northern Iraq, under Turkish command but in coordination with the US, to occupy a 'buffer zone' up to 30 km, to be increased if deemed necessary to 40 km. On the political side, the territorial integrity of Iraq would be preserved and the Turcoman minority would be recognized as a 'foundation element' of the Iraqi nation. US forces would prevent the Kurdish militias from occupying either Kirkuk or Mosul, and the Turkish forces would also stay out of the two cities. The future political structure of the country would be one agreed to by 'all the people of Iraq', and there would be a single Iraqi national army. After intense negotiations, it was agreed that the United States would give Turkey US$6 billion in grants and US$24 billion in loan guarantees – generous, it may be argued, but still well short of the original Turkish aim.[82]

None of this could take effect until the Turkish parliament had passed a new resolution, to meet the demands of Article 92 of the constitution, but the cabinet did not reach agreement on this until 24 February. The resolution emphasized that force was seen only as a last resort, after the failure of the diplomatic option, that the presence of US troops on Turkish soil would only be temporary, and that the prevention of a massive refugee influx was a major objective. The US forces would be limited to 62,000 military personnel, 250 aircraft and 65 helicopters. The government realized that it would need to make its case as persuasive as possible, since at the beginning of February around half the cabinet still opposed the plan. Deputy Premier Ertuğrul Yalçınbayır, Speaker Bülent Arınç and President Sezer kept up an open opposition to the proposal, on the grounds that an attack on Iraq did not have international legitimacy (i.e. the clear backing of the UN Security Council).[83]

There were also signs that Erdoğan and Gül were not confident that their own backbenchers would support the resolution, although they must have thought the risk was worth taking. The opposition of the CHP was a foregone conclusion. In an interview with journalists in the Black Sea town of Rize on 12 February, Tayyip Erdoğan implied that he partially agreed with President Sezer, by saying that the government would decide on a resolution to be laid before the house 'depending on developments and a decision which the UN Security Council will make', without making it clear what would happen if there was no such decision by the UN.[84] When the resolution was brought to parliament on 25 February, Erdoğan told his party caucus that there would be no 'group decision' (equivalent to a three-line whip in the British parliament) but that the issue would be decided 'by persuasion'.[85] Because the government leaders were having difficulty in doing this, they then decided to postpone a vote on the resolution until 1 March, to follow a meeting of the National Security Council on 28 February. Evidently, their expectation was that since the NSC could be taken as representing the views of the military, and since the military had hitherto backed the US plan (even if reluctantly) and had given a favourable response at the NSC's previous meeting on 31 January, it could be expected to give a positive recommendation which would win round the reluctant AKP deputies.[86]

The criticism of this tactic was that the government was trying to evade its responsibility, and shift the burden of what it knew would be an unpopular decision onto the shoulders of the generals. If this was so, then it failed to pay off. In fact, at this late stage the Turkish military were reported to be worried about US plans to pass on heavy weapons to the Kurdish *peshmergas*, increasing the risk of a 'war within a war' between the Turkish army and Kurdish militias. This was a serious cause of concern for the Turkish military, which had tried to ensure that any arms distributed to the *peshmergas* should be collected back after the war against Saddam was over.[87]

On 26 February the influential columnist Fikret Bila, writing in the Istanbul daily *Milliyet*, reported that, according to what he later described as a 'very high-ranking commander', the generals might well urge that passage of the resolution be delayed, until this problem was cleared up. On the following day, the General Staff secretariat firmly denied this report, stating that 'the Turkish Armed Forces have always avoided behaviour which could influence the free will of the Grand National Assembly [the official title of the Turkish parliament]'.[88] Critics were entitled to argue that this hardly corresponded to the army's attitudes on crucial occasions in the past. Instead of issuing a clear message of support for the resolution, as the government had hoped, the NSC meeting of 28 February failed to produce any definite recommendation. According to one account, President Sezer remarked that the NSC had already made its views known at its previous meeting on 31 January: the final decision rested with parliament, and no new recommendation was needed. Neither the military commanders, nor Gül and the other ministers present objected to this effectively.[89] Accordingly, the brief official statement issued after the meeting merely said that the results of the negotiations with the US had been 'evaluated', without issuing any recommendation.[90] Later, General Özkök repeated the view that the military had not wanted to be seen as influencing the democratic will of parliament.[91] To put it more crudely, it appeared that the Generals were as reluctant as the politicians to take responsibility for an unpopular move.

This indecision disappointed the government since, as Vecdi Gönül, Minister of Defence, later admitted, it increased the doubts of reluctant backbenchers.[92] Nevertheless, the government went ahead, by submitting the resolution to a closed parliamentary debate on 1 March. Evidently, it decided that its large majority would probably suffice to carry the day, and that it was anyway too late to back out now.[93] In fact, the vote in parliament, in an anonymous electronic ballot, produced a knife-edge result, with 264 deputies supporting the motion, 250 opposing, nineteen abstentions and thirteen absentees. It was calculated that some sixty-eight AKP members voted with the opposition, with another thirty-one casting abstentions or absenting themselves. Government leaders later suspected that a number of deputies, who had previously pledged their support, voted 'no' when they were faced with the stark decision as to whether they could support a war which both they and their constituents opposed.[94] According to one account, three cabinet ministers who had signed the draft resolution actually voted against it in the ballot, with another abstaining.[95] Although the 'yes' votes outnumbered the 'no's, parliament's rules required that, for the motion to carry, a majority of the deputies present in the house would need to vote in favour, but the total doing so was just three short of this.[96] Turkey thus escaped direct involvement in the Iraq war by no more than a hair's breadth.

Needless to say, the rejection of the plan caused much bitterness and anger in the Pentagon, where it had not been expected. Paul Wolfowitz described the parliament's decision as a 'big, big mistake'.[97] In an interview with the Turkish television station CNN-Türk on 7 May 2003 he argued that Turkey had been prepared to 'seemingly do deals' with Saddam Hussein, and urged 'let's have a Turkey that steps up and says "We made a mistake"'. He also criticized the Turkish military for not having played a 'leadership role', by failing to endorse the invasion plan on 28 February.[98] For the State Department, Colin Powell, who had not been an outspoken supporter of the plan, attempted to defuse the row this produced by saying that he did not think Turkey had anything to apologize for, although the US had suffered disappointment, and that he expected relations with Turkey to continue and strengthen in the future.[99]

On the Turkish side, Tayyip Erdoğan rejected the charge that Turkey had made a mistake,[100] but he and his colleagues were still left without a clear policy on Iraq, and evidently worried that they might be left with no influence over the post-war situation. To try to avoid this, they were prepared to table a second resolution, which might go some way to meeting US demands. However, they appeared to believe that they still had some time before the US launched an invasion of Iraq. They were also preoccupied with the change of government following the Siirt by-election which, by coincidence was scheduled for 9 March (see p. 89). Hence, they postponed a new approach to parliament until after the new government under Tayyip Erdoğan received a vote of confidence on 18 March. It was not until after the Azores summit on 16 March, and President Bush's announcement of the following evening that Saddam Hussein would have forty-eight hours to leave his country or face certain war, that the Turkish government apparently realized the urgency of the situation, and not until 20 March, several hours after the invasion of Iraq had begun, that another resolution was submitted to the parliament in Ankara. This was passed by the substantial majority of 332 votes to 202, with one abstention. However, it fell well short of the original US agenda, since it merely allowed the US and Britain the use of Turkish airspace to attack Iraqi targets from carrier-based air forces in the Mediterranean or long distance bases in Britain – something which all other NATO countries allowed. It also authorized Turkish forces to enter Iraq 'to exercise an effective deterrent force' (against whom was unstated) – the one part of the original plan on which the US was least enthusiastic.[101]

The passage of the resolution did not by itself decide the future Turkish role in Iraq, since there was still the possibility that Turkish forces might cross the Iraqi frontier. It was only on 21 March 2003 that the Turkish negotiators backed down, and agreed to the modalities of the US use of Turkish air space without insisting on a substantial Turkish military presence in northern Iraq. To add to the sense of crisis, there were reports that Turkey had sent a force of 1,500 commandos over the border near Çukurca, in Hakkari province, in the early hours of 22 March.[102] This was denied by the Turkish General Staff, but provoked a sharp response in Western capitals, as Colin Powell, Donald Rumsfeld and the British defence minister Geoff Hoon all made it clear that they opposed any Turkish advance into Iraq.[103] The effect was to tell Turkey that it could not have its cake and eat it. Since it had not allowed US forces to open a 'northern front', it could not expect to have any substantial military presence in Iraq, and must learn to cope with the consequent situation.

Notes

1. For a detailed account, see Richard C. Campany, Jr., *Turkey and the United States: The Arms Embargo Period*, New York: Praeger, 1986.
2. Mark Parris, 'Allergic Partners: Can US–Turkish Relations be Saved?', *Turkish Policy Quarterly*, vol. 4, no. 1, 2005, p. 1.
3. Daniel Pipes, in a round-table discussion chaired by James Glazov, 'Turkey: the Road to Sharia?', *FrontPageMagazine.com*, 6 May 2005 <www.frontpagemagazine.com>, p. 3.
4. Michael Rubin, in ibid., p. 6.
5. Under the Turkish constitution, general elections must be held at least once every five years. However, parliament can vote to hold early elections by a simple majority (the Prime Minister does not have the right to dissolve parliament unilaterally).
6. Interview with Mrs Ecevit (who was officially Deputy Chair of the DSP) in *Milliyet*, 15 May 1999.
7. Ibid., 30 June 1999. See also Ayten Gündoğdu, 'Identities in Question: Greek–Turkish Relations in a Period of Transformation (1)' *MERIA Journal*, vol. 5, no. 1, 2000.
8. See Hande Paker, 'Particularistic Interactions: State (In)Capacity, Civil Society, and Disaster Management', in Fikret Adaman and Murat Arsel, eds, *Environmentalism in Turkey: Between Democracy and Development?*, Aldershot and Burlington VT, Ashgate, 2005, pp. 282–5; Paul Kubicek, 'The Earthquake, Europe, and Prospects for Political Change in Turkey', *MERIA Journal*, vol. 5, no. 2, 2000, pp. 2–4.
9. For the details, see Ergun Özbudun and Serap Yazıcı, *Democratization*

Reforms in Turkey (1993–2004), Istanbul, Turkish Economic and Social Studies Foundation [TESEV], 2004.

10. *Briefing* (Ankara: weekly) 26 Feb. 2001, pp. 3, 6, 8 and 10: website of NTV television, Istanbul <www.ntvmsnbc.com> 19 Feb. 2002.

11. An example was an incident reported in October 2001 when Derviş, then in Washington, was evidently having difficulty in persuading the IMF to release the next tranche of agreed credit, or extend new loans. On 5 October he made a direct approach to Vice President Dick Cheney, following which the IMF agreed to a new standby agreement. See Bülent Aliriza, 'Turkey and the Global Storm', *Insight Turkey* (Istanbul: quarterly) vol. 3, no. 4, 2001, p. 33.

12. For a summary of the 2001 crisis, and the following IMF-backed recovery programme, see *Country Profile 2005: Turkey*, London, Economist Intelligence Unit, 2005, pp. 38–9. Other data from ibid. p. 71.

13. See reports in *Hurriyet*, 4 May 2002: NTV website, 13, 17 and 27 May, and 10 June 2002; *Radikal*, 10 June 2002; *Briefing*, 10 June 2002, p. 2.

14. NTV website, 31 July 2002.

15. Under Article 312 of the then Turkish Penal Code.

16. For more detailed accounts of Erdoğan's career up to 2002, see Metin Heper and Şule Toktaş, 'Islam, Modernity and Democracy in Contemporary Turkey: The Case of Recep Tayyip Erdoğan', *Muslim World*, vol. 95, no. 2, 2003, pp. 157–85; Ruşen Çakır and Fehmi Çalmuk, *Recep Tayyip Erdoğan: Bir Dönüşüm Öyküsü*, Istanbul, Metis, 2001, esp. pp. 9–111 and 183–95; Bilal Çetin, *Türk Siyasetinde bir Kasımpaşalı; Tayyip Erdoğan*, Istanbul, Gündem, 2003, passim.

17. *Hurriyet*, 11 Dec. 2002.

18. NTV website, 2 Dec. 2002.

19. Ibid., 11 and 12 Mar. 2003.

20. *Briefing*, 22 Nov. 1999, pp. 7 and 28, and 29 November 1999, p. 3: *International Herald Tribune*, 22 Nov. 1999.

21. Anatolia Agency, 11 Sept. 2001.

22. NTV website, 10 Oct. 2001.

23. *Hurriyet*, 20 June 2002: Murat Yetkin, *Tezkere: Irak Krizinin Gerçek Öyküsü*, Istanbul, Remzi, 2004, p. 39.

24. Mark R.Parris, 'Turkey and the US: A Partnership Rediscovered', *Insight Turkey*, vol. 3, no. 4, 2001, p. 4.

25. Quoted, *The Economist* (London: weekly) 11 Oct. 2001.

26. *Radikal*, 7 Nov. 1998.

27. Yetkin, *Tezkere*, pp. 11–15. In 1996 the Iraqi National Accord (INA), which largely consisted of Iraqi military personnel who had defected from Saddam Hussein's regime and was led by Iyad Allawi, had attempted a coup d'état against Saddam Hussein, with the covert support of British intelligence and the CIA (the so-called 'Silver Bullet' coup). The plot failed, since the INA's military network within Iraq had been penetrated by agents loyal to Saddam.

Those involved in Iraq were rounded up by the regime and executed: see Scott Ritter, *Iraq Confidential: The Untold Story of America's Intelligence Conspiracy*, London, I. B. Tauris, 2005, pp. 163–7. Following the overthrow of Saddam in 2003, and the United States' handover of sovereignty to the interim Iraqi government in June 2004, Allawi became Prime Minister of Iraq. He retained this post until April 2005, after Iraq's first post-Saddam parliamentary elections.

28. Yetkin, *Tezkere*, pp. 24 and 27–8.

29. Ibid., pp. 21 and 30–2; *Radikal*, 16 July and 29 Sept. 1999.

30. Yetkin, *Tezkere*, pp. 28–9.

31. Aylin Şeker Görener, 'US Policy towards Iraq: Moral Dilemmas of Sanctions and Regime Change', *Turkish Review of Middle East Studies* (Istanbul: annual) vol. 12, 2001, p. 43.

32. Christopher Meyer, *DC Confidential*, London: Weidenfeld & Nicolson, 2005, pp. 161–2, 220, 236–7 and 250.

33. Interview with Sir David Frost on BBC World Television, 18 December 2005, from BBC News website (http://newsvote.bbc.co.uk).

34. Interview on CNN-Türk television, 21 Sept. 2001: reported in *Radikal*, 22 Sept. 2001.

35. Bill Park, *Turkey's Policy towards Northern Iraq: Problems and Perspectives*, London: Routledge, for International Institute for Strategic Studies, Adelphi Paper 374, 2005, p. 23.

36. See the statement by Faruk Loğoğlu, the Turkish ambassador in Washington, in *Defense News*, Nov. 2001, quoted in *Briefing*, 26 Nov. 2001, p. 10.

37. NTV website, 5 Dec. 2001: *Hurriyet*, 6 Dec. 2001.

38. These 'red lines' were specified in a memorandum drawn up by the Turkish Foreign Ministry in August 2002: see Fikret Bila, *Sivil Darbe Girişimi ve Ankara'da Irak Savaşları*, Ankara: Ümit Yayıncılık, 2003, pp. 166-71 and Appendix 3.

39. Yetkin, *Tezkere*, pp. 39–40: *Briefing*, 21 Jan. 2002, pp. 3–4: *Radikal*, 17 Jan. 2002.

40. NTV website, 20 Mar. 2002: *Radikal*, 21 Mar. 2002.

41. *Briefing*, 4 Feb. 2002, p. 8: NTV website, 9 Feb. 2002.

42. *Radikal*, 6 Sept. 2002.

43. See, e.g. *New York Times*, 12 Sept. 2002.

44. *The Economist*, 3 Oct. 2002. In September 2002, Taha Yassin Ramadan, Iraq's Deputy President, was reported to have told a visiting group of Turkish journalists that the Iraqi people would fight alongside 'our Kurdish brothers' to keep Turkish troops out of northern Iraq: ibid.

45. Yetkin, *Tezkere*, pp. 51 and 63–6: Bila, *Sivil Darbe*, pp. 144–9 and Appendix 1.

46. Yetkin, *Tezkere*, pp. 74 and 81.

47. Bila, *Sivil Darbe*, pp. 183–90 and 192, and Appendix 5.

48. Ibid., pp. 170, 177, 220 and 238: Bill Park, 'Turkey, the United States and Northern Iraq', in Paul Cornish, ed., *The Conflict in Iraq, 2003*, Basingstoke and New York NY, Palgrave Macmillan, 2004, p. 80.
49. Bila, *Sivil Darbe*, p. 182.
50. Park, 'Turkey, the United States and Northern Iraq', pp. 82–3. See also Ibrahim al-Marashi, 'Iraq's Constitutional Debate', *MERIA Journal*, vol. 9, no. 3, 2005, p. 149.
51. Yetkin, *Tezkere*, pp. 77, 82 and 84–6; *Radikal*, 22 Oct. 2002.
52. Meyer, *DC Confidential*, pp. 261–2.
53. AKP election manifesto, 1992: *Herşey Türkıye İçin;Ak Parti Seçim Beyannamesi*, p. 84 (from AKP website <www.akparti.org.tr>).
54. Text from <http://daccessdds.un.org/doc/UNDOC/GEN/NO2/682/26>.
55. That is to say, the European Council decided that if Turkey implemented the improvements in human rights demanded by the EU by December 2004, then accession negotiations would begin 'without delay' after that date. In December 2004 the Council fixed a starting date of October 2005, which was just achieved.
56. *Hurriyet*, 13 Dec. 2002.
57. Park, 'Turkey, the United States and Northern Iraq', p. 81.
58. Yetkin, *Tezkere*, pp. 99–101 and 112.
59. Philip Robins, 'Confusion at Home, Confusion Abroad: Turkey between Copenhagen and Iraq', *International Affairs*, vol. 79, no. 3, 2003, p. 561.
60. Yetkin, *Tezkere*, pp. 109 and120: Bila, *Sivil Darbe*, pp. 196–7; *Turkish Daily News*, 11 Dec. 2002.
61. Nasuh Uslu, Metin Toprak, İbrahim Dalmış, and Ertan Aydın, 'Turkish Public Opinion towards the United States in the Context of the Iraq Question', *MERIA Journal*, vol. 9, no. 3, 2005, Tables 1 and 2.
62. Yetkin, *Tezkere*, pp. 116–17; Bila, *Sivil Darbe*, p. 198.
63. Meeting of the National Security Council on 28 December: *Milliyet*, 29 Dec. 2002.
64. NTV website, 24 Jan. 2003.
65. Yetkin, *Tezkere*, pp. 83–4, 127–8, 131–2 and 143–4; *Hurriyet*, 12 Feb. 2003; Bila, *Sivil Darbe*, p. 217.
66. Quoted, *The Economist*, 16 Jan. 2003.
67. Ibid.
68. *Hurriyet*, 31 Jan. 2003.
69. *Radikal*, 5 Feb. 2003.
70. Ibid., 7 Feb. 2003.
71. *Turkish Daily News*, 11 Feb. 2003.
72. *The Independent* (London: daily) 10 Feb. 2003: NTV website, 11 Feb. 2003.
73. Yetkin, *Tezkere*, pp. 151–8: *Hurriyet*, 20 Feb. 2003.

74. Yetkin, *Tezkere*, pp. 158–9: Robins, 'Confusion at Home', p. 563: *Radikal*, 15 and 16 Feb. 2003.
75. *Hurriyet*, 5 Dec. 2002.
76. Bill Park, 'Between Europe, the United States and the Middle East: Turkey and European Security in the Wake of the Iraq Crisis', *Perspectives on European Politics and Society*, Leiden, Brill, vol. 5, no. 3, 2004, p. 499.
77. Quoted, ibid., p. 500.
78. NTV website, 24, 25 and 26 Feb. and 7 Mar. 2003.
79. Yetkin, *Tezkere*, pp. 146–7.
80. *Zaman*, 29 Dec. 2005.
81. Yetkin, *Tezkere*, p. 151.
82. Ibid., p. 171. For the text of the memorandum on military aspects, see *Milliyet*, 22–25 Sept. 2003, and Bila, *Sivil Darbe*, Appendix 7. Other details from *Hurriyet*, 21 and 26 Feb. 2003: *Radikal*, 28 Feb. 2003: NTV website, 27 Feb. 2003: *The Economist*, 1 Mar. 2003.
83. Yetkin, *Tezkere*, pp. 147 and 151: *Hurriyet*, 18 and 27 Feb. 2003: NTV website, 25 Feb. 2003. For the text of the resolution, see Yetkin, *Tezkere*, pp. 163–5, and Bila, *Sivil Darbe*, Appendix 6.
84. NTV website, 12 Feb. 2003.
85. Ibid., 25 Feb. 2003.
86. Yetkin, *Tezkere*, pp. 167–8.
87. Park, *Turkey's Policy*, p. 25.
88. Fikret Bila, 'Uçaksavarlar Kime?', *Milliyet*, 26 Feb. 2003, and '"Kürtlere silah" krizi sonunda bitti!', ibid., 27 Feb. 2003. I am very grateful to Şahin Alpay for bringing this to my attention. For a later and fuller account, see Bila, *Sivil Darbe*, pp. 226–8.
89. Yetkin, *Tezkere*, pp. 168–9.
90. *Hurriyet*, 28 Feb. 2003.
91. NTV website, 5 Mar. 2003.
92. *Hurriyet*, 18 May 2005 (interview with Vecdi Gönül).
93. According to Fikret Bila, Gül and Erdoğan previously estimated that about forty of their backbenchers would defect (Bila, *Sivil Darbe*, p. 230) but this should have left the government with a fairly comfortable majority.
94. Information from Alan Makovsky, who visited Ankara with a delegation from the US Congress soon after the vote.
95. *Radikal*, 2 Mar. 2003: Yetkin, *Tezkere*, pp. 172 and 177–8. Fikret Bila relates that Deputy Prime Minister Ertuğrul Yalçınbayır stated that although he had signed the bill in cabinet, he would vote against it in the house. More controversially, Bila also suggests that Gül himself was among those who had reservations about the plan, and that it was a 'widespread opinion' that had he tried harder he could have persuaded parliament to support it. Gül's worries were said to be based on the fact that the AKP's grassroots were against the plan, and that since he was only a temporary Prime Minister, pending

Erdoğan's election to parliament, he could not take responsibility for such a momentous decision (Bila, *Sivil Darbe*, pp. 225–6 and 233). Against this it should be pointed out that Gül never made any public statement to that effect, and evidently played his part in trying to persuade AKP backbenchers to support the resolution.

96. I.e. the total number in the house was 533: a majority of this would have been 267.
97. Quoted, Daniel Pipes, 'Turkey's Radical Turn?' *New York Post*, 5 Aug. 2003.
98. Quoted, *Briefing*, 12 May 2003, pp. 1–2.
99. NTV website, 7 May 2003.
100. *Briefing*, 12 May 2003, p. 3.
101. Ibid., 20 Mar. 2003.
102. NTV website, 22 Mar. 2003.
103. Ibid.; *Sunday Times* (London) 23 Mar. 2003; *The Times* (London) 22 Mar. 2003; *Hurriyet*, 22 Mar. 2003.

FIVE

The Aftermath, 2003–5

The Turkish parliament's rejection of the 'northern front' plan left Turkish policy towards Iraq in disarray, with little influence on events in Iraq, and critical tensions in its relations with Washington. Over the next twenty-two months, numerous attempts were made to patch up the relationship, but these failed to overcome the distrust on both sides, which reached a high point around the end of 2004. By February 2005, however, it appeared that a turning point had been reached. With the political reconstruction of Iraq emerging, Turkey came to see that it could play a positive role in Iraq's future, and that the gap between Turkish and US policies was a relatively narrow one. A developing relationship between Baghdad and Ankara reduced the tension with Washington. Clearly, the alliance had suffered serious damage, but it was now being repaired in a new environment.

Trials and Tribulations: April 2003–January 2005

In the aftermath of the shock caused by the parliamentary vote of 1 March 2003, Secretary of State Colin Powell paid his first visit to Ankara since December 2001 on 2 April. He told journalists that 'we are looking for a spirit of accommodation', although he admitted that the 1 March vote had been disappointing for the US.[1] Afterwards, Abdullah Gül, who had taken over as Foreign Minister in the new government, went so far as to claim that the visit had 'strengthened our relations and helped to dispel all issues with regard to relations between the two countries'.[2] Sober reflection suggested that this was far from the case, and that the events of March 2003 had set up serious conflicts between Turkey and the US, producing crucial alterations of the regional power balance. Until March 2003, the US had depended on Turkey (and notably the İncirlik air base) to contain Saddam Hussein from the north, giving the Turks some leverage over American policy in Iraq. Now that American forces were in occupation of Iraq itself, and Saddam Hussein was removed from power, the US had no need of the Turkish stepping stone. The change was symbolized by the withdrawal from İncirlik of the US war planes, previously tasked with the enforcement of 'Northern Watch'. In effect, Turkey largely lost such ability as it had previously possessed to develop an independent policy in Iraq.[3] Around 1,500 Turkish troops of the Special Forces – essentially a left-over of previous Turkish military interventions of the 1990s – remained in northern Iraq, but they only had a marginal influence over the course of events. As the British scholar Bill Park concluded in 2004, 'in the wake of the US invasion, and with a tightening Kurdish grip on northern Iraq, the Turks have been largely on the outside looking in, seemingly without a clearly defined policy'.[4] Unfortunately, it took them some time to develop an effective one.

For the Kurds of Iraq the outcome of 2003 could be seen as a best case scenario, since it removed the hated Saddam Hussein and kept the Turkish army out of their territory. Since they were the only group in Iraq which firmly supported US policy, and had substantial forces on the ground which Turkey lacked, it was the Iraqi Kurds, rather than the Turks, who emerged as America's most effective local allies, at least in the short run. The fear that, in return, they would demand independence, or something close to it, as well as control of the oil resources of Kirkuk, and that the US might agree to this, became the dominant concern for Turkish policy makers. Some Turkish critics believed that the US had no intention of trying to keep Iraq together, but would be happy to see it break up into separate states, in accordance with a 'divide and rule' strategy. This would include an independent Kurdish republic in the north under American protection, although US government leaders persistently denied this.[5] Meanwhile, the perceived failure of Turkey to live up to its billing as America's 'strategic partner' was reflected in the American media, as well as reactions in the Pentagon. As a writer in the *Boston Globe* claimed in April 2003,

> from the outset, the behaviour of the Kurds has been the model of an ally, and the behaviour of the Turks has been the model of the opposite – unacceptable for a fellow NATO member and borderline suicidal for a new and shaky government facing a mountain of economic woe.[6]

This view may have been exaggerated, and was not reflected in official statements by the US government, but it contained a large grain of truth, causing grave worries in Ankara.

In the wake of Colin Powell's visit to Ankara, some attempts were made to patch up the Turkish–US relationship, and ease tensions with the Iraqi Kurds. On 24 June the government issued a decree allowing the US the use of the İncirlik base for one year, as well as the ports of Mersin and İskenderun, for logistical support of coalition operations in Iraq.[7] In return for the opening of Turkish air space, and the use of overland routes through Turkey to supply the US forces in northern Iraq as well as civilian consumers with needed supplies, Turkey received a credit line from the US worth US$8.5 billion, although in the event this was never used. More immediately, during April–May 2003, there were revived contacts between Ankara and both the PUK and KDP, with a view to preventing future conflicts, as well as renewed assurances from President Bush that the US would prevent the foundation of an independent Kurdish state in Iraq.[8] Unfortunately, these developments were overshadowed by sharp conflicts on the ground. On 10 April, immediately after US forces had taken over Baghdad, Kurdish forces entered Kirkuk, effectively overstepping one of Turkey's 'red lines', and it was apparently only after a threat by Abdullah Gül that Turkish forces would intervene if the US failed to do so that American troops entered the city.[9] This was succeeded by a far more open and bitter clash on 4 July 2003 when eleven soldiers of the Turkish Special Forces stationed in Suleimaniyah, in the southern part of Iraqi Kurdistan, and some local Turcomans were arrested by US troops, disarmed and detained with sacks over their heads. They were officially described as having been involved in 'disturbing activities' (in the words of the US State Department) and even having been involved in a plot to murder the Governor of Kirkuk, according to Jelal Talabani.[10] Donald Rumsfeld later expressed his 'regret' over the affair,[11] but it caused widespread protests in Turkey, especially in the army, with General Özkök claiming that it represented 'the biggest crisis of confidence' between Turkey and the US.[12] It also led to renewed warnings to Turkey by the EU, the US and Britain not to intervene militarily in northern Iraq.[13]

In spite of these conflicts on the ground, the summer and autumn of 2003 also saw fairly sustained efforts by both the Turkish and US governments to heal the wounds, primarily by including Turkish troops in the 'stabilization force' (officially international, but actually overwhelmingly American) which was attempting to restore order and suppress attacks by pro-Ba'thist terrorist insurgents in post-Saddam Iraq. On the Turkish side, the hope evidently was that a Turkish presence in the stabilization force would give Turkey some leverage over events in Iraq, and help to assuage anger in Washington over parliament's rejection of the 'northern front' plan.[14] For the US military, it was also expected to relieve some of the pressure on their own forces, and show that a democratic Muslim nation supported them in Iraq. Unofficial approaches on this started as early April as 2003, although it was not until 20 July that Tayyip Erdoğan announced that the US had made this request. This was confirmed by Colin Powell during a visit to Washington by Abdullah Gül on 24 July.[15] Initially, both sides seemed to be keen on the idea in principle, although there were differences over what the status of a Turkish contingent would be, what it would do, and where it would be stationed. While an important objective from the Turkish side was to deploy a counterweight to the Iraqi Kurds, the US was anxious to keep Turkish forces out of northern Iraq, so as to avoid clashes with the Kurdish militias. By 6 September, however, it had apparently been agreed that the Turkish contingent would have its own command, and a designated area of operations, probably in the Sunni Arab area west of Baghdad. Turkey would command a force of one division, or 10,000–12,000 troops, but of these only two brigades (6,000–8,000 troops) would be Turkish, with the third brigade expected to be from Pakistan.[16] Had the plan gone through, then Turkey would have had the third biggest national contingent in the stabilization force, after the British.

To put this commitment into action, another resolution authorizing the dispatch of Turkish troops abroad had to be put through parliament. Since the deputies in Ankara could convince themselves that this could not be construed as aggression against Iraq, and would (it was hoped) restore some of Turkey's influence in the country, it encountered far less parliamentary opposition than the previous resolution of 1 March had done. Accordingly, a motion authorizing the dispatch of Turkish troops to Iraq for one year, with the functions and composition of the force and the timing of the operation left to the government to decide, was passed by the house on 7 October 2003 with the ample majority of 358 votes to 183.[17] By this stage, however, it was clear that the idea would be strongly opposed within Iraq – not only by the Kurds, but also the Arab Shi'ites who account for the majority of the population, as well as some of the Sunni Arabs. During August and early September, there were visits by Iraqi delegations (mainly Sunni Arab) to Turkey, and a Turkish delegation to Iraq, which reportedly favoured the idea.[18] Against this, and although it had been nominated by the US authorities in Iraq, the Iraqi Provisional Governing Council clearly opposed it. The Council was supported in this by Paul Bremer, Administrator of the Coalition Provisional Authority.[19] Hence, the Turkish parliament's resolution was immediately rejected by the Governing Council.[20] In Washington, Paul Wolfowitz maintained that 'we are the ones who make the decisions'[21] – by implication, not the Iraqis – but it was clear that the opposition of the Governing Council as well as the American administrators in Iraq, who appeared to be in conflict with the Pentagon on this point, had stymied the proposal. By 23 October 2003 it was being reported that the US government had shelved the plan. On 6 November, following a telephone conversation between Gül and Powell, it was announced that Turkey had withdrawn its offer, with American agreement.[22]

This outcome left some hard-liners on the Turkish side disappointed, since they had hoped that a military presence in Iraq could be used to put pressure on both the US and the Iraqi Kurds. On the other hand, there had been substantial public opposition in Turkey to the idea of any Turkish military involvement in Iraq, and appreciation of the dangers which Turkish peacekeepers would probably face.[23] Most Turks probably thought they had had a lucky escape from being sucked into a quagmire in Iraq. At the same time, Turkey had shown its goodwill towards the US (or at any rate, to those on the US side who favoured the proposal). As one member of the Turkish parliament put it 'We will have made our gesture to the Americans and come away without paying the price ... it will be a win-win situation for the government and the Turkish people' – the opposite of that of 1 March 2003.[24]

Another effort to rebuild bridges between Ankara and

Washington derived from the fact that Turkey was the only country in the region with a Muslim population and a democratic government. One of the proposals of the neo-conservatives in Washington was that the overthrow of Saddam Hussein's regime would be the first step in a grand project for the political reconstruction of the Middle East. Under the 'Democratic Domino' theory, following the establishment of democratic government in Iraq, repressive regimes in the region would collapse one by one.[25] The first clear step in this direction was the 'Middle East Partnership Initiative' announced by Colin Powell in December 2002.[26] Eric Edelman, the US ambassador in Ankara, described the project as 'America's most important strategic initiative'.[27] Turkey could act as an important support for this ambitious project, it was thought. In principle, the idea was not without its supporters in Turkey, even though they would have preferred that the US be detached from it. Independently, Abdullah Gül took a separate initiative in championing the cause of political reform in the region in May 2003, when he told a meeting of Foreign Ministers of the Organization of the Islamic Conference in Tehran that 'it is time for all the Muslim countries to look at ourselves' and that they must act with a new vision based on reason, transparency, basic rights and freedoms, and the equality of men and women.[28] There is no evidence that Gül had not acted on his own initiative, and he pointedly avoided linking his call for reform to US strategies, which would almost certainly have destroyed its credibility in the minds of most of his audience.

The theme was taken up again by President Bush, in a visit to Istanbul for a NATO summit at the end of June 2004. By this stage, it was clear that the US was in serious difficulties in Iraq, and that it would probably do best to shift attentions to the grander vision of regional democratization. Against the dramatic backdrop of Istanbul's Ortaköy mosque and the Bosphorus suspension bridge, the President told his audience at Galatasaray University that 'the historic achievement of democracy in the broader Middle East will be a victory shared by all', that 'your country, with 150 years of democratic and social reform, stands as a model to others', and that 'we're thankful for the important role that Turkey is playing as a democratic partner in the Broader Middle East Initiative'.[29] In reaction, Turks were likely to conclude that Bush's proposals sounded fine in terms of general principles, but it was sometimes hard to match them with the American record in Iraq (such as the Abu Ghraib prison scandal, or later the attack on Fallujah) or to say what the 'Broader Middle East Initiative' was supposed to amount to in practical policy terms.

Turkey's parallel involvement in the global campaign against terrorism came back onto the top of the agenda in November 2003, when a series of suicide bomb attacks on two synagogues, a British bank and the British Consulate in Istanbul, killed a total of around fifty-five people, including the British Consul, and injured another 750. The attacks were evidently the work of ultra-Islamist terrorists, connected with al-Qaida, and provoked a series of arrests, mostly of Turkish citizens, including several suspects who were returned to Turkey from Syria.[30] They caused shock and expressions of solidarity from around the world, with messages of condolence and condemnation from Pope John Paul II, and the Prime Ministers of Britain, Greece and Italy, as well as visits by the British Foreign Secretary Jack Straw, and the German Foreign Minister Joschka Fischer. In Washington, President Bush and the US Congress both strongly condemned the attacks, and there were declarations on both sides that the Turkish–US alliance was as strong as ever.[31]

Nonetheless, the terrorist threat was also the cause of tension between Ankara and Washington, mainly because around 5,000 members of the PKK continued to be holed up in camps in northeastern Iraq after their organization had largely been suppressed in Turkey at the end of the 1990s. The US, like most Western countries, accepted that the PKK was a terrorist organization. However, its military commanders in northern Iraq were extremely reluctant to suppress it, since they evidently did not want to provoke conflict with the Iraqi Kurdish leaders, or stir up trouble in the one part of the country which was relatively peaceful and pro-American. In September 2003 the PKK, which went through a number of official name changes during 2002–5 but was almost universally referred to by its old title, officially ended the ceasefire which it had declared in 1999 (p. 69).[32] Thereafter attacks on Turkish military and gendarmerie posts were resumed, as well as terrorist killings of innocent civilians (many of them children who stepped on mines laid by the PKK). By July 2005 the campaign had cost nearly 150 lives, including those of thirty-seven civilians.[33] The failure of the US to suppress the overt presence of the PKK in Iraqi territory naturally led to bitter complaints by the Turkish side that America was applying double standards: it was expecting Turkey to cooperate against al-Qaida and other organizations which attacked American targets (as it was doing in Afghanistan) but refused to suppress an equally dangerous organization which had Turkish targets in its sights, or to allow Turkish forces to enter Iraq to do the job themselves.[34]

In July 2003, under some pressure from Washington, the Turkish parliament passed what was known as the 'Return to Society Law' under which people who had been members of the PKK but had not actually participated in acts of violence would be pardoned. Others, except for the top leaders of the organization, would be granted reduced sentences if they turned themselves in.[35] This was expected to clear the ground for an offensive against the PKK in Iraq by the US forces in the spring of 2004, but it failed to achieve its objectives. Instead, the deal was rejected by the PKK leaders, who demanded a full amnesty. By the beginning of September 2003 around 2,000 people had applied to benefit from the new law, but almost 90 per cent of them were already in prison in Turkey. Only a handful had come in from Iraq, where the PKK evidently still exercised a tight control over its followers.[36] As a result, no action was taken by the US forces in Iraq. In August 2004 Condoleezza Rice, then President Bush's national security advisor, said that the US was trying to combat the PKK, but apparently by non-military means, leaving the Turkish side quite unconvinced. Hence, by the end of 2005, Turkey had made virtually no progress on this issue.

The future of the İncirlik air base was another contentious question on the Turkish–US agenda, now that the occupation of Iraq had ended the 'Northern Watch' operation. In August 2004 the Bush administration announced plans for a global re-deployment of its forces, withdrawing 100,000 troops from Western Europe and East Asia and moving some to regions where post-cold war conflicts were judged more likely to erupt. This was expected to include re-deploying about fifty F-16 war planes from Spangdahlen, in Germany, to İncirlik.[37] As such, it provoked worries in Turkey, on the grounds that the US sought to avoid restrictions on their use once the F-16s were re-deployed, possibly allowing the US to use them for attacks against third countries with which Turkey had no disputes: such deployment would in any case require parliamentary authorization, under Article 92 of the constitution, unless it could be justified as part of Turkey's NATO commitments, which seemed unlikely.

It was not until the following year that this question was settled. On 12 January 2005 the US Central Forces (CENTCOM) commander, General John Abizaid, visited Ankara, and proposed that İncirlik be made available for direct 'operational uses' of an unspecified nature, with an increase in the number of US planes stationed there. Douglas Feith, US Under-Secretary of Defense for Policy, followed General Abizaid with another visit to Ankara for talks on this issue on 2 February 2005. By this stage, it was being reported that Washington had given up its plans to re-deploy F-16s from Germany to İncirlik, which would be used purely as a 'logistics base and rotation centre' – effectively the role which the Turkish government had agreed to in June 2003. This was confirmed in May 2005, when President Sezer endorsed a cabinet decree allowing the US and other coalition forces to use İncirlik for logistical support of operations in Iraq and Afghanistan, provided this was limited to the transfer of personnel and 'non-lethal' equipment.[38] This sticking point between Turkey and the US had thus been removed, although it was clear that İncirlik's strategic importance to the US had been much reduced since the days of the cold war, and the 'Provide Comfort' operation in Iraq.

During 2003–4, Turkey's relations with other Middle Eastern countries – notably Israel and Syria – also troubled its relationship with Washington. On the first score, the breakdown of the Israeli–Palestinian peace process in the failed 'Camp David II' negotiations of 2000, the subsequent election of Ariel Sharon as Israel's Prime Minister and the start of the 'second *intifada*' in the occupied territories, had inevitably weakened the Turkish–Israeli entente established in 1996, since it made it far more difficult for Turkey to maintain good relations with both Israel and the PLO simultaneously. This had already become apparent under the Ecevit government in April 2002, when the Prime Minister had described Israeli attacks on PLO positions in the West Bank as a 'genocide against the Palestinian people', causing counter-protests from the US Congress.[39] In March 2004 the killing from an Israeli helicopter of Sheikh Ahmad Yassin, the spiritual leader of the militant Palestinian organization Hamas, was sharply criticized by the Turkish foreign ministry, as well as the UN Secretary-General Kofi Annan, the British Foreign Secretary Jack Straw, and the EU Commission. Tayyip Erdoğan went so far as to describe the killing as a 'kind of terrorism', although he also condemned Hamas as a terrorist organization.[40] The killing of more than forty Palestinians demonstrating against Israel's military drive into the Rafah strip in May 2004 was also criticized by Erdoğan as 'developments reaching the point of terror[ism] by states'.[41] As a reaction, on 8 June Turkey briefly recalled its two senior diplomats from Tel Aviv 'for consultation'.[42]

Later in June 2004, further arguments erupted when the journalist Seymour M. Hersh reported in the *New Yorker* magazine that Israeli agents had been training Kurdish commandos in northern Iraq. The Turkish government was evidently disturbed by this, reportedly on the grounds that the same commandos might be used by the Kurds to attack targets in Turkey. While the Israeli ambassador in Ankara denied that Israel would do anything in northern Iraq without asking Turkey, Abdullah Gül stated that if the story were true then there would be a heavy price to pay.[43] Nor was the atmosphere improved when the Israeli daily *Haaretz* complained that on 13 July Erdoğan had refused to meet the visiting deputy premier of Israel Ehud Olmert, on the grounds that he was on holiday, when he had actually received the Syrian Prime Minister Muhammad Naji al-Utri on the same day.[44] By the end of 2004, however, the tension had considerably relaxed, following the death of Yasser Arafat and the beginnings of tentative (if unsuccessful) moves towards peace in Palestine. On 3–5 January 2005 Abdullah Gül visited both Israel and the West Bank territories, laying a wreath at the holocaust memorial in Yad Vashem, and promising help for the reconstruction of Gaza after the expected Israeli withdrawal. Previous Israeli criticisms, which had never been as shrill as those of some of Israel's supporters in the US,[45] were forgotten: in fact *Haaretz* spoke of the 'deep affection that each country's people feels for the other' and criticized 'the erroneous approach ... that Turkey needs Israel, due to the latter's ties with Washington, more than Israel needs Turkey'.[46]

While Turkey's disputes with Israel had some damaging effects on its relationship with Washington, its relations with Syria had a similar impact, but for the opposite reason – that Ankara was developing cooperative links with a country with which the Bush administration was at loggerheads. Since Hafiz al-Assad's expulsion of Abdullah Öcalan from Syria in 1998, and the succession to the Syrian presidency of his son Bashar in 2000, the Syrian government was active in removing points of conflict with Turkey, including virtually shelving its claim to the province of Alexandretta (Hatay), annexed by Turkey in 1939, and dropping complaints over the distribution of the waters of the Euphrates (pp. 33–4). Along with Iran (another member of President Bush's 'axis of evil') Syria joined Turkey in opposing the idea of an independent Kurdish state in Iraq. The new atmosphere of amity was symbolized by an official visit to Ankara by Bashar al-Assad in January 2004, and a return trip to Syria by Tayyip Erdoğan the following December. On the latter occasion the two countries signed a free trade agreement, and the dispute over the Euphrates seemed to have been laid aside, to the extent that Turkey offered to pump water from the Tigris into Syria, at the point where it flowed along the Syrian border.[47] However, a major crisis between Syria and the Western powers began in February 2005, with the murder of the Lebanese Prime Minister Rafik Hariri, which was widely blamed on Syria, and the subsequent passage of UN Security Council Resolution 1559, co-sponsored by the United States and France, calling for the withdrawal of all Syrian forces from Lebanon. The Syrian government also came under attack from Washington for sponsoring terrorism in Iraq. The crisis affected Turkey, since on 14 April President Sezer paid a long pre-arranged visit to Damascus. Prior to the visit, Ambassador Eric Edelman gave an interview in Bursa which was misinterpreted as constituting pressure on the government to scrap or postpone it. Nonetheless, it went ahead, with the Turkish government stressing that the President had emphasized to his Syrian hosts the need to withdraw their troops from Lebanon by the end of April 2005.[48]

While the most serious points of direct friction between Turkey and the US derived from events in northern Iraq, 2004 also saw a deterioration in the psychological atmosphere between the two countries, caused mainly by sharp criticisms by the Turkish press and politicians of the way the US forces were handling their task, and exaggerated anti-American conspiracy theories in parts of the Turkish media. The Americans, like the Israelis, came under verbal fire as their attempts to restore authority in Iraq caused serious civilian casualties: in fact, in May 2004 Tayyip Erdoğan linked his accusation of 'state terrorism' against Israel to US bombings of civilian targets in Iraq.[49] Tensions re-erupted in November 2004, following the US attacks on Fallujah, in which over 2,000 people were reported to have been killed. Deputy Mehmet Elkatmış, the Chairman of the Turkish parliament's Human Rights Commission, went so far as to accuse the US of 'genocide of the Iraqi people'.[50] For the government, Abdullah Gül was more cautious, saying merely that 'we are telling American officials everything which we find wrong' and accused the US of 'excessive use of force'. Tayyip Erdoğan also described those who had been killed in Fallujah as 'martyrs'.[51] Apparently to express his displeasure and the misgivings in his own party about US policies in Iraq, the Prime Minister kept Ambassador Edelman waiting for an appointment for six weeks, until 13 December 2004, causing further complaints in the American press.[52] Meanwhile, pro-Islamist sections of the Turkish media produced elaborate conspiracy theories to suggest that the war in Iraq was part of a US–Jewish–Israeli plot to dominate the Middle East, and even (for instance) that the American bombing in Iraq in May 2003 had been responsible for an earthquake in the eastern Turkish province of Bingöl.[53]

Overshadowing this war of words were continuing wrangles between Turkey and the US over the status of the Kurds within a reconstructed Iraq and, in particular, the future of Kirkuk. The Transitional Administrative Law which was issued in Iraq in

March 2004, pending the adoption of a permanent constitution, recognized the Kurdistan Regional Government (KRG) as the official authority in the three ethnically Kurdish provinces of northern Iraq, with the *peshmergas* allowed to function as the internal security force within this zone. In Kirkuk, with its conflicting mix of Kurds, Arabs and Turcomans, an interim authority with representatives of all these communities, but dominated by the Kurds, was set up under US auspices in May 2003. However, the city was left outside the zone officially controlled by the KRG. Under Article 58 of the Law, the 'permanent resolution' of the city was to be postponed until a permanent constitution was ratified and a 'fair and transparent census has been conducted'.[54] Nonetheless, Kurdish leaders, especially Massoud Barzani, made it clear that their aim was to include it in a Kurdish state, either within or outside Iraq. To support this claim, there was a mass return of Kurdish families who had been expelled from Kirkuk during a ruthless process of 'Arabization' by Saddam Hussein's government since the 1970s, at the expense of Arabs who had been moved in to replace them.

The 'Kurdification' of Kirkuk was also resisted by the local Turcomans, who claimed it as their ancestral home, and some of whom looked to Turkey for support.[55] Tensions between Ankara and Washington over the position of the Turcomans reached a high point in September 2004, when US and Kurdish forces attacked the largely Turcoman town of Tal Affar, claiming that it had been taken over by insurgents from Syria. Abdullah Gül threatened that if the attack were not halted, then Turkey would cease any cooperation with the US over Iraq. Later, the two sides agreed to combine in providing humanitarian aid to the inhabitants, and the Turcomans were left responsible for its security. By this stage, however, it was apparent that the Turkish-sponsored Iraqi Turcoman Front (pp. 76, 100) did not have monopoly support of the Turcoman community. In fact, the Turcomans were quite divided politically: some 40–60 per cent of them were estimated to be Shi'ite rather than Sunni Muslims, and many identified themselves with Arab Shi'ite groups, or with other ethnic parties, rather than the ITF. Others doubted the nationalist credentials of the ITF, given that it was sponsored by a foreign power.[56]

For the Turks, the future of Kirkuk came back onto the top of the agenda in January 2005, in the run-up to Iraq's first democratic elections for a Transitional National Assembly, held on 30 January. In the days before the election, both the Turkish General Staff and Prime Minister Erdoğan warned that Kurdish attempts to rig the vote in Kirkuk by bringing in Kurds from other districts would make the results questionable and that, in Erdoğan's words, 'the US and other coalition forces ... will have to pay for the negative events that could happen in the future'.[57] Just before the elections, Massoud Barzani raised the temperature further by declaring that 'Kirkuk is a Kurdish city with a Kurdish identity. An independent Kurdish state will be established, but when it will be established I don't know'.[58] According to the published results, Kurdish parties won 68 per cent of the vote in Kirkuk, but the Turkish press claimed that this was because in the previous week 110,000 Kurds had been moved into the area to vote. Simultaneously, the Kurdish leaders organized an unofficial referendum in Iraqi Kurdistan, from which it was claimed that there was a 95 per cent majority in favour of independence.[59] Erdoğan reacted to these events with a very thinly veiled attack on the US, telling the AKP parliamentary caucus that 'unfortunately, those forces which say that they have come to the region in order to bring democracy have preferred to remain insensitive to these anti-democratic ambitions'.[60] By this stage, it was clear that the Turkish government was sharply at odds with the US over its policy in Iraq, but not at all clear what alternative strategy it would propose.

Re-orientations: February–December 2005

Although few could probably have predicted it at the time, the crisis in Turkish–American relations at the time of the Iraqi elections in January 2005 turned out to be a turning point. By the end of the year, the worst of the bitterness between the two countries seemed to have been softened, and there was even a respectable degree of convergence in Turkish and American policies towards Iraq. Three developments appear to have contributed to this. The first was the apparent recognition by the Turkish media and government that they could not allow exaggerated criticism of the US to get out of hand, and that what could broadly be called public relations had an important role to play in improving the environment for diplomacy. Secondly was the definite progress which Turkey made in achieving its ambition of eventually gaining full membership of the European Union. While the causal connection was hard to prove, this improvement almost certainly helped to shift Turkish attention from the Middle East to Brussels, making it easier for Turkey to take a broader view of the Iraqi problem. Thirdly, and most importantly, Turkish–Kurdish relations improved, and the Bush administration produced a road-map for the gradual transfer of power to an elected Iraqi government. By the end of the year, this still had an uncertain outcome, but the Ankara government had come round to the realization that Turkish and American plans and preferences were not that far apart, and that it would do best to give the road-map cautious support.

On 5–6 February 2005 Condoleezza Rice paid her first visit to Ankara as Secretary of State in George W. Bush's second administration. This was an important opportunity to patch up the relationship, and her discussions with Foreign Minister Abdullah Gül were described as having been 'extremely beneficial and positive'.[61] However, soon afterwards, the relationship suffered a rude shock from an article by one of the paper's editorial team, Robert J. Pollock, headlined 'The Sick Man of Europe – Again' which appeared in *The Wall Street Journal* on 16 February 2005. If journalists ever wish to show the power of the press – for good or for ill – in international politics, then Pollock's article would serve as a good example. On the face of it, it seemed unlikely to bring about an improvement in Turkish–American relations, since the burden of its argument was a fierce counter-attack against wildly overblown and often irresponsible reporting on Iraq, and US policy in general, in the Turkish media. In Pollock's view 'the common thread is that almost everything the US is doing in the world – even tsunami relief – has malevolent motivations'. His most serious complaint was that 'in the face of such slanders Turkish politicians have been utterly silent'. Turks appeared to have forgotten all that the US had done for them in the past, such as opposition by successive administrations to anti-Turkish motions in the Congress over the Armenian massacres during the Frst World War, strong support for Turkish membership of the EU, or vital intelligence help in the arrest of Abdullah Öcalan in 1999.

Pollock's conclusions from this seemed excessively gloomy. He complained, for instance of the 'intellectual decadence of much of Istanbul's elite' and concluded that:

> much of Ataturk's legacy risks being lost, and there won't be any of the old Ottoman grandeur left either. Turkey could easily become just another second-rate country: small minded, paranoid, marginal.

Nonetheless, the reaction in Turkey was not entirely hostile, even among those who were not supportive of US policy in Iraq, or its foreign policy in general. As an example, İsmet Berkan, editor of the liberal daily *Radikal*, while describing the article as 'not easy to swallow', admitted that:

> an important part of the widespread anti-American discourse [in Turkey], as *The Wall Street Journal*'s writer has said, derives from paranoia, and we support this paranoia in our newspapers ... whether we like it or not, it gives rise to some doubts about the mental health of the society in which we live, and will continue to live.[62]

The gist of Pollock's message was repeated, albeit in much more moderate tones, by Douglas Feith, whom Pollock had accompanied on his visit to Turkey for the talks on İncirlik at the beginning of February. Answering a question from a Turkish journalist at a meeting at the Council of Foreign Relations in Washington on 17 February, Feith argued that:

> When you're talking about relationships between democratic countries, it's crucial that the appreciation of those relationships extend beyond government officials down to the public in general, because otherwise the

relationship is really not sustainable ... we hope that the officials in our partner countries are going to be devoting the kind of effort to building popular support for the relationship that we build in our own country.[63]

These remarks were interpreted by one Turkish journalist as 'It's an order: everyone is to love America!'[64] However, the evidence was that Turkish leaders were indeed anxious to bring down the temperature. Addressing the AKP parliamentary caucus on 23 February, Tayyip Erdoğan adopted a quite different tone from that of the previous month, urging that:

differences between countries which can understand one another cannot be the cause of serious tension just because of speculations by some circles ... we are still expecting the coalition forces which are in Iraq will restore peace and stability.[65]

Thereafter, critics in the Turkish press softened their rhetoric on America, and the issue appears to have dropped off the political agenda.

A paradoxical feature of Turkey's foreign relations during 2004–5 was that, while its alliance with the US was going through a stormy period, it was making important advances in its path towards membership of the European Union. In January 2004 Tayyip Erdoğan reversed his predecessors' hard-line policy on Cyprus, which went back almost thirty years, by accepting the plan produced by the United Nations Secretary-General, Kofi Annan, as the basis for a settlement on the island. Sadly, this was rejected by the Greek Cypriots in a referendum held on 24 April 2004, although accepted by the Turkish Cypriots. The Cyprus problem thus remained unresolved, but at least Turkey was able to show that it had done everything it could to remove this obstacle, thus helping to clear the way for the start of accession talks with the EU. Erdoğan's government also took important steps to comply with the 'Copenhagen criteria' of democratic norms stipulated by Brussels – most notably in May 2004, when parliament passed a raft of constitutional amendments designed to broaden human rights generally and expand the cultural rights of the Kurds.[66] Turkey received its reward at the meeting of the European Council held in Brussels on 16–17 December 2004, when the heads of state and government of the EU member countries agreed to start accession negotiations with Turkey in October 2005, provided certain conditions, notably regarding Cyprus, were met. After these were sufficiently implemented, and after much last-minute haggling, the EU leaders accepted the formal start of accession negotiations on 3 October 2005. Although there were many potential pitfalls ahead, Turkey now had an important new perspective for a revised foreign policy strategy, in which concentration on narrow nationalist concerns, such as those over Iraq, could be replaced by a broader and more liberal, more supra-national vision.

As a reflection of this, in an article in *Radikal* on 25 February 2005, Deniz Zeyrek reported that the Ankara foreign policy establishment was working towards 'breaking the taboos' which had previously limited its options. These included a new approach to relations with Armenia and policy towards Cyprus, and a thorough reconsideration of the red lines which had previously governed Turkey's attitude towards Iraq and the Iraqi Kurds. The latter had included sharp opposition to a Kurdish takeover of Kirkuk or the granting of autonomy to the Kurds within a federal republic of Iraq, while protecting the rights of the Turcomans. Instead, Turkey needed to give priority to the establishment of a democratic regime in Iraq as a whole, as well as securing the stability and territorial integrity of the country. It should strengthen its relations with the Shi'ites of Iraq, as the biggest group in Iraqi society. The Iraqi Turcomans should be encouraged not to isolate themselves from the rest of the country, but instead to play an active part in the national politics of Iraq. At a press conference on 17 February 2005, a Foreign Ministry spokesman had given a signal of all this by saying that 'our approach to Iraq is strategic: it cannot be reduced to [the question of] Kirkuk'.[67] The overall criticism of Turkey's previous policies appeared to be that they had been too narrow and purely reactive. Instead, Turkey needed to be more proactive and long-sighted, with a broader vision, not limited to the local power struggle in northern Iraq.

This new approach did not produce immediate results, or fully overcome the substantial points of difference between Turkey and the US. The point became clear on 7–8 June 2005, when Tayyip Erdoğan visited Washington for an hour's talk with President Bush, among other engagements. His main aim was to try once more to persuade the US government to suppress the PKK bases in northern Iraq. On this score, no visible progress was made, although Erdoğan stated that he had been told that unspecified steps would be taken against the PKK, and the White House confirmed that it regarded it as a terrorist organization.[68] On a more positive note President Bush repeated the message he had given at Galatasaray University just one year before, describing Turkey as a role model for more democratic government in the Middle East, and calling on Turkey to take a lead in his 'Broader Middle East Initiative'.[69]

Erdoğan was evidently willing to take up this relatively cost-free way of improving his relationship with Washington. However, while Turkey was happy to promote the cause of democracy in the region, and the reduction of tensions between the Muslim world and the West, it preferred to dissociate this from US strategies.

More concretely, Turkey's policies towards Iraq, and hence its relations with the US, were bound to be affected by a de-escalation of Turkey's internal Kurdish problem, if this could be achieved. If the Kurdish community in Turkey could be persuaded that its best course of action would be to seek more liberal treatment within the Turkish republic, rather than support violence or seek a solution by joining up with the Iraqi Kurds, then Turkish suspicions of the Iraqi Kurdish leadership, and hence potential clashes with the US, could be significantly reduced. In October–November 2004 a controversial report on 'Minority Rights and Cultural Rights' was issued by the Human Rights Advisory Board, which is attached to the Prime Minister's Office. This suggested that Kurdish citizens should be allowed to refer to themselves as 'from Turkey' (*Türkiyeli*) rather than 'Turkish' (*Türk*), echoing Tansu Çiller's stillborn suggestion of December 1994 that 'Turkish citizen' should be an accepted alternative identity (p. 68).[70] For foreign observers, this debate must have seemed abstract and esoteric, but for Turkey it had a crucial importance. As Will Kymlicka remarked in 1995, 'the problem is not that Turkey refuses to accept Kurds as Turkish citizens. The problem is precisely its attempt to force Kurds to see themselves as Turks'.[71] The report provoked a heated public debate, with the government washing its hands of it, declaring that it had not commissioned it, but at least another chapter seemed to have been opened in Turkey's long-running Kurdish problem. What also became apparent was that the AKP's previous promotion of the idea of 'Islam as a cement' between Turks and Kurds had not had much effect.[72]

On 9 November 2005 an unexpected opportunity to carry this debate forward occurred when a bomb exploded outside a bookshop in the town of Şemdinli, in the remote province of Hakkari, killing two bystanders and injuring another thirteen. What made the attack special was the strong evidence that it had been planted by local gendarmerie officers, acting as an undercover hit squad.[73] Rather than trying to sweep the incident under the carpet, Tayyip Erdoğan ordered a full investigation. He visited the town on 21 November, assuring his local audience that Turkey would not be based on ethnic nationalism, and would accept all ethnicities and cultures. Kurds should be free to call themselves Kurds, their primary identity being that of citizens of Turkey, with their secondary identity Kurdish.[74] In effect, Erdoğan had taken the official discourse back to the point where Tansu Çiller had left it in January 1995 – the big difference being that he enunciated it much more clearly, and had a far better grip on governmental power. Hence, although Erdoğan was criticized, he did not retract his statement. What remained to be seen was whether his government could translate this change of principles into concrete policies. On this score, there was some forward movement in the following months, notably a long-delayed decision to allow private television companies to broadcast in Kurdish, beginning in March 2006.[75] Nevertheless, the people of the south-east were still left with many serious material grievances, which still had to be addressed.[76]

These changes had important potential implications for Turkey's policies towards Iraq since, if it could become more confident of the loyalty of its own Kurdish citizens, then it could approach the likely devolution of power within Iraq with more equanimity. In effect, the 'Sèvres syndrome' would lose its force. Crucial in this was the emergence of new political structures and prospects in Iraq. Following the elections to the Transitional National Assembly of Iraq in January 2005, Jelal Talabani was elected President of Iraq in the following April. This was of fundamental importance in Turkey's Iraq policy, since it meant that one of the two main Kurdish leaders had a position of power in Baghdad. Turkey strongly supported this, since if they had a fair share of power in the central government, then the Iraqi Kurds would be far less likely to opt for independence. Reversing previous policies, the Turkish government now accepted that Iraq would be a federal republic, with a substantial degree of autonomy for the Kurds.[77] Realistically, it had to admit that it had never had the right to tell the Iraqi people what sort of constitution they should have, but Talabani's election made this change of direction much easier to swallow. It was also made easier by the fact that, from the start, Talabani admitted that an independent Kurdish state would not be viable: in fact, he later conceded that it would be 'only a dream'.[78] Presumably reflecting instructions from Ankara, the Iraqi Turcoman Front announced that it would fully support the new President.[79] In sharp contrast with his earlier criticisms of the Iraqi elections, Erdoğan now conceded that they had been 'a turning point for the history of that country' and 'an important stage for the Iraqi people to reclaim their own political processes and future'.[80]

A further stage in this process was marked on 20 May 2005 when Ibrahim al-Ja'aferi visited Turkey for his first trip abroad since taking office as Prime Minister of Iraq in the previous month. On two crucial points, al-Ja'aferi assured Erdoğan that he would not allow 'any group in Iraq [implying, the PKK] to damage the security of neighbouring countries' and that the 'territorial integrity and political unity of Iraq' should be protected.'[81] Although it was not clear how al-Ja'aferi's government could, by itself, ensure the first objective, his basic message naturally came as music to Turkish ears.

The next important stage in the political reconstruction of Iraq was the issuing of a draft constitution, which was put to a national referendum on 15 October 2005. Three features of the draft were reassuring to Ankara. First, contrary to the original Kurdish proposals, none of the new 'regions' of Iraq (of which Kurdistan was obviously the most critical) had the right to secede. Secondly, Article 109 of the draft stated that 'oil and gas is the property of all the Iraqi people in all the regions and provinces'. Thirdly, Article 149 extended the formula provided for by Article 58 of the previous Transitional Administrative Law for an interim administration in Kirkuk until a proper census could be held: this would have to take place by 31 December 2007 at the latest.[82] These provisions did not allay all the Turkish government's worries. For example, there was no proof that the local Kurdish leaders could not settle enough of their own people in Kirkuk to ensure that it would eventually be attached to the Kurdistan region, at the expense of the other communities in the city. There were also worries that the Kurds might exploit a clause in the constitution (Article 110/1) providing that regional governments as well as the national administration would be responsible for managing oil and gas extraction, so as to allow them to control any new oil fields.[83] However, the hope was that the new Iraqi parliament would agree to constitutional changes on these and other crucial points. Hence, Abdullah Gül and others strongly supported the referendum on the new constitution.[84]

While Jelal Talabani was playing a very positive role from the Turkish viewpoint, the same was not necessarily true of Massoud Barzani since, as President of the Kurdistan Regional Government, he appeared to have less interest in preserving Iraq's unity, and still occasionally talked of declaring independence.[85] Nonetheless, the Ankara government decided it would be best to tackle him head-on. Hence, on 20 October 2005, the head of Turkey's National Intelligence Organization (MİT) Emre Taner met the KDP leader for exploratory talks in Arbil. While these were supposed to be secret, news of them leaked out, with Barzani admitting they had taken place some six weeks later. What had been decided was not clear, although it appeared that Barzani had asked to be allowed to pay an official visit to Turkey in 2006 (itself an encouraging sign) and may have given assurances that he would not try to break away from Iraq.[86] This was evidently in preparation for a visit by Barzani to Washington on 25 October. His reception ruffled feathers in Ankara, since he was addressed by George W. Bush as 'Mr President', causing the Turkish Foreign Ministry to ask what state he was supposed to be President of (how else he should have been addressed was unclear). However, the important advance from Ankara's viewpoint was that he joined Bush in declaring support for the territorial integrity of Iraq, adding 'we are realists, not suicidally inclined nationalists'.[87] This degree of policy alignment between Turkey, the US and the Iraqi parties was developed further on 4 December 2005, in the run-up to Iraq's second round of parliamentary elections, when Abdullah Gül hosted a meeting in Istanbul with Ambassador Zalmay Khalilzad, Tariq al-Hashemi of the Iraqi Islamic Party, and the leaders of two other Sunni Arab parties in Iraq. The object, which was apparently achieved, was to convince the Sunni parties not to boycott the elections, as they had in the previous January, and demonstrated further Turkish support for the hoped-for new order in Iraq.[88]

Needless to say, these developments did not remove all the resentments in Ankara and Washington caused by parliament's rejection of the 'northern front' plan on 1 March 2003. As late as December 2005, Donald Rumsfeld was still complaining that if US troops had been allowed to invade Iraq from the north, then the resistance in the Sunni triangle of western Iraq could have been defeated far more easily[89] (that the US forces had had over two and a half years since then to deal with the problem was evidently ignored). Nonetheless, the fact that there was now a degree of convergence between Turkish and US policies, with both governments supporting the reconstruction of Iraq as a democratic federal state, meant a distinct improvement in the relationship. Some of this may also have been due to changes at the top in Washington, as two of the most powerful champions of neo-conservatism and an aggressive unilateralist policy in the Middle East, Paul Wolfowitz and Douglas Feith, both left office in the summer of 2005.[90] As Secretary of State, Condoleezza Rice seemed to have a much better grip on the overall direction of US foreign policy than her predecessor, Colin Powell, and was keen to rebuild relationships which had been badly damaged by the Iraq war.

Notes

1. Website of NTV television, Istanbul <www.ntvmsnbc.com> 2 Apr. 2003; *Economist Global Agenda* <www.economist.com/agenda> 2 Apr. 2003.
2. Associated Press, 3 Apr. 2003.
3. Ziya Öniş and Şuhnaz Yılmaz, 'The Turkey–EU–US Triangle in Perspective: Transformation or Continuity?', *Middle East Journal*, vol. 59, no. 2, 2005, p. 277.
4. Bill Park, 'Iraq's Kurds and Turkey: Challenges for US Policy', *Parameters*, vol. 34, no. 3, 2004, p. 26.
5. For Turkish comments to this effect, see, e.g., International Crisis Group, *Iraq: Allaying Turkey's Fears over Kurdish Ambitions*, Brussels, International Crisis Group, Middle East Report No. 35, 26 Jan. 2005, p. 14.
6. Thomas Oliphant, 'A Lesson for Turkey from Kurdish Allies', *Boston Globe*, 13 Apr. 2003; quoted in Cengiz Çandar, 'Turkish Foreign Policy and the War on Iraq', in Lenore G. Martin and Dimitris Keridis, eds, *The Future of Turkish Foreign Policy*, Cambridge MA and London: MIT Press, 2004, p. 53.
7. *Hürriyet*, 24 June 2003.
8. NTV website, 29 Apr., 30 Apr. and 8 May 2003.
9. Murat Yetkin, *Tezkere: Irak Krizinin Gerçek Öyküsü*, Istanbul, Remzi, 2004, pp. 206–7.
10. Ibid., pp. 220–2; *Hürriyet*, 5 and 8 July 2003; NTV website, 7 and 8 July 2003.
11. NTV website, 15 and 17 July 2003.
12. Quoted, Bill Park, 'Between Europe, the United States and the Middle East: Turkey and European Security in the Wake of the Iraq Crisis', *Perspectives on European Politics and Society*, Leiden: Brill, vol. 5, no. 3, 2004, p. 501.
13. Öniş and Yılmaz, 'The Turkey–EU–US Triangle', p. 276.
14. See the statement by Abdullah Gül, in *Hürriyet*, 8 Aug. 2003.
15. Yetkin, *Tezkere*, pp. 214–15; NTV website, 21 and 24 July 2003.
16. NTV website 14 and 19 Aug., and 4 and 6 Sept. 2003; *Hürriyet*, 27 Aug., and 4 and 7 Sept. 2003; *Turkish Daily News*, 23 Aug. 2003: *Zaman*, 5 Sept. 2003; Yetkin, *Tezkere*, pp. 214–16, 234 and 242–4; Bill Park, *Turkey's Policy towards Northern Iraq: Problems and Perspectives*, London: Routledge, for International Institute for Strategic Studies, Adelphi Paper 374, 2005, p. 37.
17. NTV website and *Hürriyet*, 7 Oct. 2003.
18. NTV website, 27 and 28 Aug., and 10 Sept. 2003.
19. Ibid., 24 Oct. 2003: *The Economist* (London: weekly) 18 Oct. 2003; Michael Rubin, 'A Comedy of Errors: American–Turkish Diplomacy and the Iraq War', *Turkish Policy Quarterly*, vol. 4, no. 1, 2005, p. 5. Rubin writes that Bremer 'was furious' over the Turkish parliament's vote and 'instructed his governance team to provide reasons why Turkish troops should not enter Iraq': he also claims that Bremer had personally played a role in the arrest of

the Turkish soldiers in Suleimaniyah on 4 July 2003 (ibid.).

20. *Hürriyet*, 7 Oct. 2003.
21. Quoted, Yetkin, *Tezkere*, p. 251.
22. *Radikal*, 23 Oct. 2003; *Financial Times* (London) 8 Nov. 2003.
23. See Nasuh Uslu, Metin Toprak, İbrahim Dalmış, and Ertan Aydın, 'Turkish Public Opinion towards the United States in the Context of the Iraq Question', *MERIA Journal*, vol. 9, no. 3, 2005, p. 5. A poll conducted in September 2003 found that 64 per cent of respondents opposed sending Turkish forces to Iraq, while 31 per cent were in favour.
24. Quoted, *The Economist*, 18 Oct. 2003. Kemal Kirişçi comes to the same conclusion, describing the outcome as a 'win-win situation' for the Turkish government: Kemal Kirişçi, 'Between Europe and the Middle East: The Transformation of Turkish Policy', *MERIA Journal*, vol. 8, no. 4, 2004, p. 5.
25. Liam Anderson and Gareth Stansfield, *The Future of Iraq: Dictatorship, Democracy or Division?*, Basingstoke and New York: Palgrave Macmillan, 2004, pp. 185–6.
26. Katerina Dalacoura, 'US Democracy Promotion in the Middle East since 11 September 2001: A Critique', *International Affairs*, vol. 81, no. 5, 2005, p. 964.
27. Quoted, *The Economist*, 22 Jan. 2004.
28. *Turkish Daily News* and *Hürriyet*, 28 May 2003.
29. 'President's Remarks at Galatasaray University', 29 June 2004: from the White House website <www.whitehouse.gov/news/releases/2004/06>.
30. See *Hürriyet*, 28 Nov. 2003; NTV website, 29 Nov. 2003; *The Economist*, 6 Dec. 2003.
31. *Zaman*, 20, 23 and 25 Nov. 2003; NTV website, 21 Nov. 2003.
32. In April 2002 it officially re-named itself as the Kurdistan Freedom and Democracy Congress (KADEK) and then, in November 2003, as the Kurdistan People's Congress (KHK). Subsequently, in 2004, it changed its name again, to the Congress for Freedom and Democracy in Kurdistan (Kongra-Gel), but by 2005 it had reverted to its original title of Kurdistan Workers' Party (PKK). To avoid confusion, it is here referred to throughout as 'PKK'.
33. *The Economist*, 21 July 2005.
34. International Crisis Group, *Iraq: Allaying Turkey's Fears*, p. 13.
35. NTV website and *Hürriyet*, 30 July 2003; *Briefing* (Ankara: weekly), 11 Aug. 2003, p. 11.
36. NTV website, 2 Sept. 2003; *Briefing*, 8 Sept. 2003, p. 9.
37. *Briefing*, 23 Aug. 2004, p. 14; *Hürriyet*, 18 Aug. 2004.
38. *Hürriyet*, 11 Jan., and 1 and 13 May 2005; *Radikal*, 12 Jan. and 2 Feb. 2005; *Turkish Daily News*, 22 Feb. 2005; NTV website 3 May 2005.
39. *Hürriyet*, 17 Apr. 2002.
40. *Hürriyet*, 22 and 25 Mar. 2004; *Turkish Daily News*, 26 Mar. 2004.

41. Ibid., 21 May 2004.
42. NTV website, 8 June 2004.
43. *Hürriyet*, 21, 22 and 23 June 2004. For Seymour Hersh's account of the affair, see Seymour M. Hersh, *Chain of Command*, London: Penguin, 2005, pp. 353–60. In December 2005 it was reported that private Israeli firms, employing retired military personnel, had been training Iraqi Kurds in 'anti-terrorism techniques', but Israeli officials were said to have assured Ankara that they were acting on their own and without Israeli government permission: *The Guardian* (London) 2 Dec. 2005; *Zaman*, 5 Dec. 2005; *Turkish Daily News*, 6 Dec. 2005.
44. *Hürriyet*, 13 July 2004.
45. See, for instance, the comments by Michael Rubin and Daniel Pipes, in a round-table discussion chaired by James Glazov, 'Turkey: The Road to Sharia?', *FrontPageMagazine.com*, 6 May 2005 <www.frontpagemagazine.com>.
46. Quoted, *Briefing*, 10 Jan. 2005, p. 8.
47. Ibid., 27 Dec. 2004, p. 3; *Hürriyet*, 6 Jan. and 22 Dec. 2004. See also Eyal Zisser, 'Syria, the United States and Iraq – Two Years after the Downfall of Saddam Hussein', *MERIA Journal*, vol. 9, no. 3, 2005, pp. 4–5.
48. *Turkish Daily News*, 14 Apr. 2005; *Radikal*, 15 Apr. 2005. For the text of Ambassador Edelman's statement in Bursa, and his subsequent explanation, see the press release from the US Embassy in Ankara of 14 March 2005, and his interview in *Vatan* newspaper of 30 March 2005, both on the US Embassy website <http://ankara.usembassy.gov>. In fact, he had merely remarked that 'we hope that Turkey will also join in that international consensus, in supporting a thorough and immediate Syrian withdrawal from Lebanon'.
49. *Hürriyet*, 20 May 2004.
50. Ibid., 25 Nov. 2004.
51. Ibid., 26 Nov. 2004; *Turkish Daily News*, 27 Nov. and 16 Dec. 2004.
52. Sedat Ergin, 'Türk-ABD ilişkileri yokuş aşağı', *Hürriyet*, 12 Dec. 2004; *Turkish Daily News*, 16 Dec. 2004.
53. Soner Çağaptay, 'Where Goes the US–Turkish Relationship?', *Middle East Quarterly*, vol. 11, no. 4, 2004, p. 2.
54. Transitional Administrative Law of 4 March 2004, Articles 53, 54 and 58: text from <www.fco.gov.uk/files/kfile/TAL>. On the interim authority in Kirkuk, see *Turkish Daily News*, 26 May 2003.
55. Park, *Turkey's Policy*, pp. 29–37.
56. Ibid., pp. 37–8; International Crisis Group, *Iraq: Allaying Turkey's Fears*, pp. 4–5 and 10–11.
57. Quoted, Park, *Turkey's Policy*, p. 34.
58. *Hürriyet*, 31 Jan. 2005.
59. Ibid., 4 Feb. 2005; NTV website, 3 Feb. 2005.
60. *Hürriyet*, 1 Feb. 2005.

61. Ibid., 6 Feb. 2005.

62. İsmet Berkan, 'Anti-Amerikanizm ve paranoya toplumu', *Radikal*, 18 Feb. 2005.

63. Transcript, 'National Defense in the Second Term', Council on Foreign Relations, Washington DC, 17 Feb. 2005: from the Council's website <www.cfr.org/publication/7858/national>.

64. Burak Bekdil, 'It's an order: Everyone is to love America!' *Turkish Daily News*, 23 Feb. 2005.

65. Quoted, *Briefing*, 28 Feb. 2005, p. 3.

66. Ibid., 10 May 2004, p. 8; *Hürriyet*, 4 May and 4 June 2004.

67. Deniz Zeyrek, 'Devlet tabu yıkıyor', *Radikal*, 25 Feb. 2005.

68. NTV website, 8 June 2005; *Hürriyet*, 10 June 2005.

69. CNN-Türk website, 9 June 2005; *Radikal*, 9 June 2005; NTV website, 9 June 2005.

70. Başbakanlık İnsan Hakları Danışma Kurulu, '*Azınlık Hakları ve Kültürel Haklar Çalışma Grubu' Raporu, Ekim 2004*, Ankara, Prime Minister's Office, Human Rights Advisory Board, 2004, p. 6. For a fuller explanation of the group's proposals, by one of its principal members, see Baskın Oran, *Türkiye'de Azınlıklar, Kavramlar, Lozan, İç Mevzuat, İçtihat, Uygulama*, Istanbul, Turkish Economic and Social Studies Foundation [TESEV] 2004, and for a detailed analysis see Ioannis Grigoriadis, *Turkish Political Culture and the European Union*, PhD thesis, School of Oriental and African Studies, University of London, 2005, pp. 289–98.

71. Will Kymlicka, 'Misunderstanding Nationalism', *Dissent*, Winter 1995, p. 132, quoted in Ümıt Cizre Sakallıoğlu, 'Historicisizing the Present and Problematizing the Future of the Kurdish Problem: A Critique of the TOBB Report on the Eastern Question', *New Perspectives on Turkey*, no. 14, 1996, p. 6.

72. *The Economıst*, 13 Nov. 2004; NTV website, 22 Oct. 2004; *Radikal*, 24 Oct. 2004; see also M. Hakan Yavuz and Nihat Ali Özcan, 'The Kurdish Question and Turkey's Justice and Development Party', *Middle East Policy*, vol. 13, no. 1, 2006, pp.103 and 111–13.

73. *Hürriyet*, 11 Nov. 2005.

74. Ibid., 21 Nov. 2005.

75. Ibid., 29 Dec. 2005. This followed the start of limited programming in Kurdish by the state broadcaster TRT in June 2004. Strictly speaking, Kurdish language broadcasting by private companies had been allowed in May 2003 (ibid., 22 May 2003) but conservative officials in the High Radio and Television Board (RTÜK) had fought a long delaying action.

76. Apart from the general economic backwardness and poverty of the region these included, most notably, the failure to return to their villages the hundreds of thousands of people who had been displaced during the fighting of the 1990s, and in many cases forcibly uprooted by the armed forces.

77. International Crisis Group, *Iraq: Allaying Turkey's Fears*, p. 8.
78. Quoted, *Hürriyet*, 9 Nov. 2005.
79. CNN-Türk website, 13 Apr. 2005.
80. Quoted, *Hürriyet*, 30 Apr. 2005.
81. Quoted, *Turkish Daily News*, 21 May 2005.
82. Text of the draft constitution from the website of the Iraqi Transitional Government <www.iraqigovernment.org>. For a detailed commentary on the constitution from the Turkish viewpoint, see Murat Yetkin, 'Irak'ın parçalanması dudurulabilir mi?', *Radikal*, 16 Oct. 2005.
83. *The Economist*, 17 Dec. 2005.
84. NTV website, 17 Oct. 2005.
85. Ibid., 18 Nov. 2005.
86. Ibid., 5 Dec. 2005; *Radikal*, 26 Nov. 2005; Yüksel Söylemez, 'Turkey's Iraq Policy, Old and New', *Turkish Daily News*, 18 Dec. 2005.
87. Quoted, NTV website, 29 Oct. 2005. On other points, see *Hürriyet*, 27 Oct. 2005.
88. *Hürriyet*, 5 Dec. 2005.
89. CNN-Türk website, 5 Dec. 2005.
90. Wolfowitz became President of the World Bank in June 2005: Feith left the Department of Defence in August, to become a Distinguished Visiting Fellow of Stanford University.

SIX

Conclusions, Assessments and Options

Seen in retrospect, the story of Turkey's relations with the United States before, during and after the invasion of Iraq in March 2003 appears as another incident like that of the dog in the night time in the Sherlock Holmes story, in that its main significance was a non-event. Turkey escaped involvement in a costly and drawn-out armed conflict, whose effects would probably have been far more damaging than the purely political clash which actually resulted. At the same time, the crisis marked a critical turning point in Turkey's alliance with the US, as well as a relationship with Iraq which stretched back to the early 1920s. Some historical determinants survived, but others were fundamentally changed. This outcome needs an explanation and assessment. The following analysis considers first the policy dilemmas which faced the Turkish government at the time, and the reasons for Turkish reluctance to support the invasion. To expand these points, the succeeding section compares the crisis with that of 1990–1, and the different results of the two experiences. This is followed by a critical assessment of both Turkish and American policy, in the light of possible alternatives. The final section considers Turkey's future options, three years after the war, and the likely effects of the story on Turkish strategies towards Iraq, the Kurds and the Western alliance.

Turkey's Policy Dilemmas and Motivations

In an illuminating article, Kemal Kirişçi has drawn attention to Turkey's situation between Europe and the Middle East, between a Kantian zone of 'democratic peace', and the Hobbesian world of autocracy, violence and conflict to its south and east.[1] Public opinion surveys have invariably shown that the big majority of Turks want their country to be incorporated into the first zone rather than the second – that they want Turkey to join the European Union, and to live in a peaceful, democratic and prosperous society, everything that the Middle East conspicuously is not. The dilemma for Turkish policy makers is that, while the United States supports Turkey's eventual accession to the European Union, its strategists value the alliance with Turkey primarily for its actual or potential role in the Middle East, the one zone which most Turks want to stay out of. This creates a clear clash between domestic political preferences and external pressures – a classic problem facing many governments in democratic countries in times of crisis. Ideally, policy-makers would like to reconcile the two, but they may not always be able to do so. Hence, they have to come down on one side of the fence or the other eventually. In February 2003 the AKP government leaders had hoped to bring parliament behind the US plan for the invasion of Iraq by emphasizing the costs of refusing it. In the end, domestic opposition proved too much for them. Looking back on it, most of them appear to have realized that they had had a lucky escape. In spite of their previous efforts to persuade parliament to accept the invasion plan, they accepted the parliamentary vote on 1 March 2003 without overt protest, and later with some relief. In fact, in April 2005 Foreign Minister Abdullah Gül effectively admitted that parliament's decision had actually been a blessing in disguise. Against this, in September 2006, Erdoğan suggested that parliament should have passed the resolution, so as to have some effect on the post-war situation: by this stage, however, it was far too late to change course.[2]

At best, at the time the government leaders were only reluctant advocates of the American plan. The reasons are not hard to find. No-one in positions of power in Turkey – in the General Staff, the Foreign Ministry, the government, the parliament or the media – actually wanted a war against Iraq, or supported the US-led invasion in principle. Saddam Hussein had very few supporters in Ankara, but Iraq was not seen as a security threat to Turkey, whether or not it still had weapons of mass destruction. On the other hand, there were serious worries that regime change by force could lead to chaos in Iraq, destabilising the whole region, and destroying the delicate power-balance between Turkey, Iran, Syria and Iraq. The popular perception that Turkey had gained nothing by supporting the US in 1990–1 – even if this was unfair – made the prospect of a second performance even less enticing. As in 1991, the argument for supporting America was based on power politics – in this case, that the Bush administration was bent on invading Iraq in any case and that on balance Turkey would be better off inside the American tent than outside it. Mistakenly, this was coupled with the idea that a Turkish troop presence in Iraq would be relatively cost-free, and would give Turkey some leverage in the post-war situation. In explaining to the press the government's reasons for its conditional support of the US plan in February 2003, Abdullah Gül did not once mention Saddam's alleged possession of mass destruction weapons: in fact he admitted that 'I do not expect any threat from Iraq, it has no power.' Instead, he based his case purely on the argument that 'we believe that our strategic partnership requires us to act together with the USA'. As he put it:

> On occasion, you have to take the most difficult decisions. We did not take this decision easily. But I, my party and government did everything [to prevent the war]. The fault has passed off our shoulders. Everyone has to think of his own country [first].[3]

Turkey's internal Kurdish problem also exacerbated Turkish worries about the likely effects of an invasion of Iraq. If the US failed to establish full control after the overthrow of Saddam Hussein, then there was every likelihood that the Iraqi Kurds would renew their bid for independent statehood. Massoud Barzani's frequent declarations before the war strengthened these expectations. After 1999, the PKK appeared to have been subdued as a paramilitary force, but many Turkish Kurds remained alienated from the Turkish state. Although it had not regained its former strength, the PKK was sufficiently emboldened by the strengthening of Kurdish power in post-Saddam Iraq to resume its campaign. Hence, Turkish attentions were focussed on the struggle for power in northern Iraq mainly because Turkey realized that it was vulnerable internally, and was worried that a political breakdown in Iraq could lead to increased violence and terrorism in its own territory. Even if Iraq held together, the army and police still had to be on their guard against the PKK.

These attitudes were reflected in public reactions to the war in Iraq of 2003. According to surveys carried out by the Turkish polling organizations Anar and Pollmark between December 2002 and September 2003, over 80 per cent of their Turkish respondents believed that the US was attacking Iraq to seize control of its oil resources or to 'show its power to the world', with less than 1 per cent believing that its main aim was to remove Saddam's alleged stock of mass destruction weapons. Another reason for opposing the war was that an invasion of Iraq without authorization from the UN Security Council would damage the United Nations, with 72 per cent of respondents agreeing to this proposition. As Muslims, the majority of Turks could be expected to have sympathy for their co-religionists in Iraq, but political pan-Islamism seems to have been a minor motive for opposing the invasion, since less than 1 per cent considered that this was a religious war.[4] Nor can Turkish opposition to the war be written down to generalized anti-Americanism. Turkey had, after all, enjoyed good relations with the United States in the late 1990s. It had fully supported George W. Bush's campaign against terrorism after 9/11, and the removal of the Taliban regime in Afghanistan. Turkish opposition to US policies started, and hopefully would end, with the war in Iraq.[5]

In the United States, some commentators in the neo-conservative camp saw the collision with Turkey as the result of a sinister conspiracy by Islamist radicals in Saudi Arabia and elsewhere to take over the Turkish government, with Tayyip Erdoğan and his colleagues their willing accomplices. They connected it to Turkey's temporary downgrading of relations with Israel in 2004, as well as its opposition to US policies in the Middle East. This argument was advanced by Michael Rubin, a resident scholar at the American Enterprise Institute, and a former adviser on Iraq and Iran in the office of the Secretary of Defense. In the spring of 2005, Rubin alleged that huge sums in 'green money' (how much was left obscure) flowed into the AKP's coffers from Saudi Arabia and Malaysia. He quoted an unnamed source to the effect that 'Saudi Arabia and Malaysia have made their foreign aid to the AKP dependent on Turkey readjusting its position toward Israel'.[6] No verifiable evidence was produced in support of these claims, and if it had been available it seemed most unlikely that the AKP's numerous opponents in Turkey, or the media, would not have brought it to light. In similar vein, Daniel Pipes suggested that Tayyip Erdoğan was 'the anti-Ataturk', out to 'undo the entire Ataturk revolution' and that this accounted for the Turkish refusal to assist the US in the invasion of Iraq.[7] The fact that the AKP government had itself tabled the motion in parliament favouring the invasion plan was conveniently ignored, as was the fact that the previous Ecevit government, most of which was strongly anti-Islamist, had been firmly opposed to the prospective invasion.

Against this, Graham E. Fuller, a former chair of the National Intelligence Council at the CIA, argued that it would be wrong 'to assume that Turkey's widespread opposition to many of the Bush administration's policies are symptomatic of a broader strategic hostility', pointing out that 'Turkey's strong secularists, nationalists, Kemalists and leftists ... are even more harshly critical of Washington than the Erdoğan government.'[8] In fact, it appeared that Rubin and Pipes or their un-named informants were inventing, or at least grossly exaggerating pan-Islamist influences, to explain an event which actually had far more simple and non-conspiratorial causes. The available evidence suggests that Turks were opposed to the war for the same reasons as millions of other people in Western Europe and elsewhere – that it was judged unnecessary, illegitimate, and disruptive. Admittedly, Saddam Hussein was a noxious tyrant, but so were many other rulers around the world, and the US was not preparing to overthrow them by force. The fact that Turkey was particularly concerned about the danger of post-war instability in Iraq made Turkish opposition more acute, but this also had virtually nothing to do with pan-Islamic radicalism, and stretched across the political spectrum in Turkey.

1990–1 and 2002–3: The Two Crises Compared

Among the criticisms levelled at the AKP government's handling of the crisis over Iraq during 2002–3 is the claim by, for instance, the journalist Cengiz Çandar, that it was far less adept than that of Turgut Özal during 1990–1. According to Çandar, the AKP leadership was amateurish and incompetent, so that Turkey lost its way in the international arena, whereas Özal was 'a visionary concerning foreign policy issues' who 'broke with the traditional reflexes to guide Turkey through the turbulent waters of international politics'.[9] Admittedly, it is hard to deny that the AKP leaders were relatively inexperienced in foreign affairs, and that they were distracted by other critical issues – notably by preparations for the European Council meeting of 12–13 December 2002, which was to decide the fate of Turkey's bid to join the EU, and the complication of arranging Tayyip Erdoğan's accession to the premiership. However, that does not prove that they were incompetent. Assessing whether Çandar's criticism is fair means comparing the two crises and the conditions which applied in each case. This comparison also brings out points which help to explain Turkish reactions on the second occasion.

On the one side, there were certainly important similarities between the two crises. On neither occasion was Iraq seen as a serious or direct security threat to Turkey, so that the argument in favour of supporting the US rested largely on the need to preserve the alliance with Washington in the post-cold war environment. Moreover, in both cases most public opinion, including a substantial part of the ruling party, opposed direct involvement in a prospective war in Iraq. On the other hand, the differences between the two experiences were also crucial. The Gulf War of 1991 had the limited aim of ejecting Iraqi forces from Kuwait. Presidents Bush and Özal may also have hoped, or expected, that defeat in Kuwait would lead to Saddam Hussein's overthrow by his own army, but they could not be sure of this, and it was not one of the coalition's stated objectives. The war of 2003 had the far more ambitious aim of regime change in Baghdad, with potentially ominous consequences for Turkey, and for the region as a whole. Moreover, the war of 1991 had an impressive degree of international legitimation, primarily in the shape of UN Security Council Resolution (UNSCR) 678 of 29 November 1990, authorizing the use of force if Iraq failed to withdraw from Kuwait by 15 January 1991. UNSCR 1441 of 8 November 2002, on the other hand, merely threatened 'serious consequences' if Saddam Hussein did not comply with his disarmament obligations. Although the British and US governments argued that this justified a war, this view was widely rejected by, among others, the UN Secretary-

General Kofi Annan (albeit at a later stage). These positions reflected the different stands taken by individual governments on the two occasions. The war of 1991 was supported by all the NATO countries and the majority of Arab states, with Russia prepared to stand aside. In 2003, however, NATO was clearly split, with France and Germany opposing the war, and nearly all the Arab countries, plus Russia, also in strong opposition. Hence, in 1991, Turgut Özal could cogently argue that in supporting the coalition Turkey was aligning itself with world opinion and UN decisions. In 2003, Abdullah Gül and Tayyip Erdoğan had no such advantage.

The two wars also differed in that Turkey was being asked to do far more on the second occasion than on the first. In 1990–1 it was merely required to enforce the economic embargo on Iraq, and to allow the US the use of its air bases. Turkish participation in the land force in the Gulf would have been welcomed by the US, but even if it had been accepted in Ankara it would probably have had no more than symbolic value. In 2003, by contrast, the Turkish parliament was additionally being asked to allow the presence of a large US land force on Turkish territory, with many Turks worried about when it would be withdrawn. By insisting that its own troops should also be allowed to enter northern Iraq, Turkey was taking on an additional risk, of the kind which General Torumtay had clearly rejected in December 1990. In effect, in 2003 the Turkish parliament was being presented with a far more ambitious, contentious and potentially dangerous agenda than in 1991. In 2003, the US government was testing the 'strategic partnership' to the limit – and, as it turned out – beyond it.

Criticisms and Alternatives

Cengiz Çandar is not alone in his sharp criticisms of the way the AKP government handled the Iraq crisis in 2002–3. For instance, the British scholar Philip Robins castigates the 'chaotic and even contradictory nature of Turkish decision-making' during this period, which he ascribes to the inexperience of the new government and its 'double-headed leadership' between November 2002 and March 2003, before Erdoğan took over the premiership. This resulted in 'confused priorities, limited attention and capacity overload'. The AKP's rise to power, he decides, may have been too rapid for its own good.[10] He is particularly critical of Abdullah Gül's attempt in January 2003 to build up a coalition of Middle Eastern nations to persuade Saddam Hussein to stand down, in which he argues that the Turkish government was simply procrastinating.[11]

Other criticisms advanced by Murat Yetkin, of the Istanbul daily *Radikal*, are that if the government leaders believed that the motion supporting the invasion plan would be passed by parliament, then they should not have tried to shift the responsibility for recommending it onto the shoulders of the military commanders, by delaying the vote in parliament until after the National Security Council meeting of 28 February 2003. If on the other hand, they believed that the motion would not pass, then they should have told the US authorities this at an early stage, and the plan would have been dropped.[12] As a former Prime Minister and President, Süleyman Demirel agrees with the second point, suggesting that if the government had tried harder, it could have had the crucial motion passed by parliament. In his view, 'If you have a one party government, you cannot simply say "this is the majority's will" ... As a matter of fact, parliaments do not rule governments. On the contrary, governments rule parliaments.'[13] The AKP government is also accused of hugely overestimating its strategic value to America, to the extent that it even convinced itself that if it refused to cooperate, then the US would be unable to act against Iraq.[14]

There are reasonable complaints that the government failed to conduct an effective 'public diplomacy' in its relations with the US, by not reacting against exaggerated criticisms of American policy in the Turkish media, and failing to present a positive image to American public opinion. In a world of instant communications, public relations were more important than Turkish government leaders apparently realized. They could naturally argue that they could not censor press comment, but they could have expressed disagreement. The upshot of this failure was the row caused by Robert Pollock's article in *The Wall Street Journal* in February 2005 (p. 141). Earlier, during January–February 2003, the prolonged haggling over financial compensation for Turkey's prospective engagement made Turkey the object of ridicule in the American media, to whom it appeared that a country which claimed to be a faithful NATO ally was actually trying to sell its support for as much money as it could get.[15] Again, the AKP government did little to effectively counter this.

Not all these criticisms seem fair, however. The government's reactions to the original US proposals may have been confused, but this was only to be expected given that little information about them had been publicly available before it came to power, and the Iraq question was just one item in a very heavy political agenda. In his Middle Eastern diplomacy during January 2003, it appears that Abdullah Gül accepted that direct approaches to Iraq would probably not succeed,[16] but the effort did have a point, since if he was to persuade his reluctant party to support a war, he had to show that he had done his best to avoid it. There may well have been some members of the government and the military who gravely overestimated Turkey's strategic importance to the US, but the claim that the government itself thought that America would not invade Iraq without Turkish cooperation does not hold water. Given that Erdoğan and his colleagues were clearly against the war, if they had really believed this, then the logical policy to pursue would have been to turn down the American plan from the start, instead of submitting it to parliament. Demirel's complaints about the government's failure to carry its own backbenchers in the 1 March vote may be met with the response that there would be no point in having parliaments in democratic countries if they merely rubber-stamped government decisions. The negotiations over financial aid created hostile reactions in America, and could have been better handled, but the government was genuinely worried about the expected economic costs of the war to Turkey, given the still-fragile state of the economy after the crash of 2001.[17] These worries were not confined to Ankara, being shared at the time by the influential weekly *The Economist* in London.[18]

Nor was US diplomacy above criticism. Policy making in Washington was largely driven by the Department of Defense, which assumed that since it had long had a close relationship with the Turkish military it could seal an agreement without having to worry about public opinion in Turkey. It was assumed that 'elite state institutions, not the masses' determined foreign policy in Ankara.[19] Key figures in Washington, like Donald Rumsfeld, Paul Wolfowitz, and Vice President Dick Cheney, had previously been regarded as 'good friends of Turkey',[20] mainly because they emphasized its strategic value, and apparently expected that this would enable them to win over the Turks without much argument.[21] On another track, Michael Rubin criticizes the State Department for its lack of high-level diplomacy in relations with Turkey, pointing out that between August 1990 and January 1991 the then Secretary of State James Baker visited Turkey four times, whereas his successor Colin Powell paid no such visits between December 2001 and April 2003. The US Embassy in Ankara, he maintains, had most responsibility for the deterioration in bilateral relations in the run-up to the war of 2003. According to Rubin, the then US Ambassador, W. Robert Pearson, had a 'tin ear for Turkish politics' and 'shirked his own responsibilities', failing to make the case for the attack on Iraq to the Turkish press, and shocking American policy makers by admitting that he had spent the day before the crucial vote of 1 March 2003 playing golf with a Turkish businessman.[22] Meanwhile, Turkey was apparently getting mixed signals from the US, mainly because American officials on the ground in northern Iraq were more worried by the prospect of a Turkish military presence than their counterparts in Washington. An example was Zalmay Khalilzad's firm opposition to this idea, evidently conveyed to the Turks, even though the combined plan was supported by the Pentagon. Later on, in the autumn of 2003 Paul Bremer strongly opposed Turkish participation in the 'stabilization force', even though this was backed by Washington at the time.[23]

Hanging over all these arguments is the question whether Turkey gained or lost in 2003 by eventually refusing to become part of President Bush's 'coalition of the willing'. As a sharp critic of the AKP and a former member of Turgut Özal's government between

1986 and 1989, Hasan Celal Güzel maintains that the rejection of the US plan on 1 March 2003 was 'perhaps the greatest mistake in the history of Turkish diplomacy', as a result of which 'Turkey was cut out of the politics of the Middle East ... Turkey's policy towards Iraq and Kurdistan has collapsed.'[24] Prior to the 1 March vote, to persuade their reluctant colleagues and backbenchers, the government leaders argued that if the plan were rejected, then the Iraqi Kurds would establish an independent state, gaining control over Mosul and Kirkuk and provoking a surge of refugees, that the US would support the Greek case over Cyprus and would withdraw its support for Turkey's bid to join the EU, and that the Turkish economy would suffer severely without the promised American support (Ali Babacan estimated that the cost of the war to Turkey within the first year would be US$23 billion, rising to US$30 billion subsequently).[25]

In the event, most of these fears proved exaggerated. In particular, Turkey's economy proved far more robust than expected. In spite of the loss of the expected US aid, there was no run on the banks or balance of payments crisis, and Turkey's GDP grew by 5.8 per cent in 2003, rising to 8.9 per cent in the following year.[26] Turkey continued to enjoy American support for its EU application and (more conditionally) its policy towards Cyprus. By the end of 2005, the risk of an independent Kurdish state being set up in Iraq, or a Kurdish annexation of Mosul and Kirkuk, seemed to have been reduced, at least for the time being. The argument that Turkey would have had important leverage over US policy in post-war Iraq if it had supported the invasion also seemed doubtful. The British government, after all, had been President Bush's most enthusiastic and consistent supporter, but had very little discernible influence over US actions in Iraq, or policy towards the Palestine question. As *The Guardian*'s columnist Simon Jenkins concluded in November 2005, 'If Colin Powell could get nowhere against the White House, what hope had Blair?'[27] – or, one could add, Tayyip Erdoğan if he had been in the same position? In the circumstances of the time, a Turkish military presence in northern Iraq threatened to lead to a dangerous and costly 'war within a war' against the Iraqi Kurds, effectively America's allies, from which Turkey would have had great difficulty extricating itself.[28]

If the AKP government's approach is judged to have been mistaken, then one also has to consider what alternatives could have been adopted. A range of options had been presented to Abdullah Gül by the General Staff on 23 December 2002 (p. 103), with complete non-cooperation at one end of the scale, allowing the US the use of ports and bases in Turkey as well as over-flight rights as intermediate positions, and full cooperation, including the participation of Turkish forces in the expected attack on Iraq, as the maximum scenario.[29] Counter-factual history is, at best, a risky endeavour, but one can risk the judgement that if the first option had been chosen, then the outcome might not have been very different from what actually resulted, the sole difference being that the Americans would at least have known where they stood from the start. One of the intermediate options – say, allowing the US air force to use Turkish air bases, as in 1991, but withholding permission for the transit of ground troops – might have softened the American reaction. However, it would still have left Washington frustrated, since the original US plan called for a large military force on the ground in northern Iraq at the start of the war. Alternatively, Turkey could have allowed the US army to use Turkish territory for an attack on northern Iraq, without demanding that Turkish troops should also be inserted. This would have met US requirements, and avoided a clash between the Turkish army and the Kurdish militias, but would have increased the risk that parliament would reject the plan, since a Turkish troop presence was thought to be an essential ingredient on the Turkish side. Finally, the Turkish government could have given full support to the invasion only on condition that it had clear UN authorization. The time to have made this clear would probably have been in November 2002, soon after the passage of UNSCR 1441, which left the question open. Had there been a follow-up resolution, a crucial part of parliamentary opposition to the plan could well have been removed. Since the US was prepared to go to war without this (a fact of which the Turks were aware) the result would probably have been similar to what actually happened, but at least part of the moral blame for this could have been shifted onto American shoulders.

All this prompts the conclusion that none of the available alternatives would have been anything like ideal. In effect, there was no 'right' answer to the question, and the Turkish government was faced with being 'damned if you do and damned if you don't'. As it happened, it probably did best by staying out of the war, but this was the result of accident rather than design.

Future Directions and Prospects: Turkey, Iraq and the US

One of the results of the turmoil in Iraq since 1990 was that Turkey had to look again at some of the ground rules which had governed its relations with Baghdad since the mid-1920s (pp. 25–7). The continuation of an approximate balance of power between Turkey, Iran, Iraq and Syria was still an important goal, as the best way of securing regional peace, but was made far more difficult by novel conditions. Some of these dangers – such as the possible development of nuclear weapons by Iran – lie outside the scope of this book. However, the serious lack of government power in Iraq since April 2003, and its heavy reliance on US forces, clearly undermined the regional balance. Respect for the frontier established in 1926 was still important, but might be hard to sustain if a power vacuum in Iraq and growing Kurdish aspirations worsened Turkey's internal Kurdish problem, as they had done in the 1990s. Events since the overthrow of Saddam Hussein also suggested that total opposition to those aspirations, and reliance on the government in Baghdad to suppress them, was no longer a viable option: Kurdish autonomy within Iraq now had constitutional legitimacy, as well as American protection.

In a penetrating study, Murat Yetkin concludes that during the crisis of 2003–4, Turkey simply had no policy towards Iraq as a whole, merely opposition to the foundation of an independent Kurdish republic.[30] As the foregoing account has shown, Turkish policy makers had seized this point by the spring of 2005. They welcomed the establishment of the new Iraqi government under Ibrahim al-Ja'aferi and the election of Jelal Talabani as Iraq's President, as well as the new constitution (albeit with some reservations). The Iraqi Shi'ites, as the dominant group in the new order in Iraq, were as keen as the Turkish government to prevent Kurdish independence, but with the difference from earlier times that the Kurds now had constitutional autonomy within the Iraqi republic. By accepting that Iraq would now have a federal constitution, the Turkish government had pulled back from its previous hard-line position, but it could live with this provided the Kurds had a fair share of power in Baghdad which would anchor them to the Iraqi state. Some commentators, like Liam Anderson and Gareth Stansfield, suggest that the best way of coping with Iraq's intense political problems would be a 'managed partition', with the Kurds forming a separate state, and the Arab Shi'ites and Sunnis either remaining together, or forming another two states.[31] Against this, Toby Dodge argues that this misjudges a complex reality, as well as underestimating the strength of a distinct Iraqi nationalism among both the Shi'ites and Sunnis, and that there are strong pressures for maintaining a single state of Iraq.[32]

The experiences of 2005 suggested that the second prediction was probably the most likely one, at least in legal or constitutional terms. By the end of that year, Iraq was still beset by government weakness, violence and terrorism, but formal partition was not being promoted as the solution. The hope was that, following the elections of December 2005, the Sunni, Shi'ite and Kurdish leaders would be able to put together a national unity government embracing all three communities, and that the US forces would stay in Iraq for long enough to re-build the Iraqi army and police, so as to maintain a tolerable degree of law and order. The Turkish government strongly supported this aim. There was a real danger, however, that this expectation would prove too optimistic, and that Iraq could collapse into civil war, or something close to it, without formal partition. When Ibrahim al-Ja'aferi paid a second visit to Ankara at the end of February 2006, it was clear that the Turkish government was well aware of this danger, but not at all clear how it could prevent it. Even if the danger were avoided, Kirkuk would continue to be a flash-point, especially if the promised census in

December 2007 resulted in its transfer to control by the Kurdistan Regional Government (p. 149). As an alternative, the Turkish government urged that Kirkuk should continue to enjoy a 'special status' within Iraq.[33]

If the reconstruction of the Iraqi state failed, then a likely outcome seemed to be continuing violence between Sunni and Shi'ite militants, with the Kurds maintaining a relatively stable hold on the north-eastern provinces. In November 2005 Massoud Barzani had claimed that if the rest of Iraq relapsed into civil war, then the Iraqi Kurds would have 'no alternative' to declaring independence.[34] Against this, Jelal Talabani argued that an independent Kurdistan could not survive, since all its neighbours (i.e. Turkey, Iran, Syria and Arab Iraq) would close its borders.[35] In fact, it seemed unlikely that Turkey would impose a complete economic blockade on Iraqi Kurdistan, since this would cause unacceptable suffering for the civilian population. On the other hand, it would almost certainly strongly oppose the declaration of an independent state by the Iraqi Kurds, and could put serious economic pressure on them short of an outright blockade – by, for instance, interrupting the flow of oil through the Kirkuk–Yumurtalık pipeline. A unilateral military intervention by Turkey seemed unlikely, although it had occasionally been threatened in the past, since it would probably be strongly opposed by the European Union as well as the United States. The abandonment of its 'European vocation' would be too heavy a price for Turkey to pay. On the other hand, Turkey might have to learn to co-exist with an Iraqi Kurdistan with something of the same status within Iraq as that formerly occupied by Montenegro within the former Yugoslavia – i.e. constitutionally part of a federal republic, but in practice separate and self-governing.

As a sign of how far Turkish thinking had travelled, by the October of 2005 the influential newspaper columnist Mehmet Ali Birand was urging his Turkish readers to think again about their future relations with the Kurds both inside and outside Iraq. Turkey, he pointed out, was the best economic lifeline northern Iraqi Kurds have ... Northern Iraq and Turkey complement each other ... In terms of security, Turkey and northern Iraq need each other ... In other words, Turkey could view the northern Iraqi Kurds not as the enemy but as a people it needs to protect.

In return, he suggested, the Iraqi Kurds could be persuaded to suppress the PKK presence in their territory and provide the Turcomans with 'living space'. Meanwhile, Turkey's own Kurdish citizens would need to be reconciled with the Turkish state through further 'socio-economic and cultural reforms'.[36] Effectively, Birand was underlining the point that Turkey's problems in Iraq were closely linked to its internal Kurdish problem. The first could not be tackled effectively without addressing the second. The nearer Turkey got to bringing more of its own Kurdish citizens into the Turkish political mainstream, recognizing their reasonable economic and cultural demands as well as basic human rights, the more confident it could be in its approach to the problems of Iraq.

Birand's proposals went ahead of the officially declared Turkish policy of the time, but they were worth considering, especially if something like the 'Montenegro scenario' became reality in northern Iraq. In the broader sphere, Turkey also needed to achieve cooperation with Iraq's other neighbours – Iran and Syria in particular – so as to prevent unilateral intervention by any of them if Iraq broke up, and ensure support for the federal government. To this end, and in the wake of escalating inter-sectarian conflicts in Iraq at the end of February 2006, Tayyip Erdoğan proposed a renewed meeting of all Iraq's neighbours. This plan had the full support of Kofi Annan, on behalf of the United Nations.[37] The fact that Iran and Syria had been included in President Bush's 'axis of evil' meant that Washington might object to this approach, but by 2006 it was clear that the President would have to soften the neo-conservative rhetoric if Iraq's chronic problems were to be addressed effectively.

Developments in Iraq, and in Turkey's policy towards it, also had important implications for its overall relationship with the US and the European Union. In the aftermath of the crisis of March 2003, it was suggested that Turkey's strengthening links with Brussels might have had a significant effect on its relations with Washington, and that there was a 'Europeanization' of Turkish foreign policy taking place.[38] As a sign of this, it was pointed out that on subjects like Iran, the Arab–Israeli conflict, and the Kyoto protocols on climate change, Turkey's policies were much closer to those of the EU than to those of the US.[39] To speak of a definite and unidirectional shift seems hard, however. 'Europeanization' implies that Turkish foreign policy would be aligned with that of Europe, however defined, when in fact, on the crucial issue of Iraq, there was no 'European' policy for Turkey to align with. In concrete terms, the construction of a common European foreign policy was still at a very early stage, and European defence structures, as distinct from NATO, still in their infancy. The inconsistencies in Turkey's relations with Europe and policies towards Iraq were equally striking. Britain, the most consistent and prominent supporter of Turkey's accession to the EU, was also Washington's closest supporter in Iraq, whereas in France the ruling party opposed both Turkish accession and the Iraqi invasion.[40] In effect, Europe was at sixes and sevens, and unable to put forward an effective or coherent alternative to American strategies.

Other conclusions were that while the Turkish–US alliance was not dead, the crisis over Iraq had shown that Washington could not count on Turkey for projection of its military power into the Middle East.[41] Hence, Turkish–US cooperation in the region would need to be based on the projection of 'soft' rather than 'hard' power, with the 'Broader Middle East Initiative' an example of this new emphasis (p. 130). The AKP government could not object to this in principle, since it offered a relatively pain-free method of restoring its relations with Washington, and it was itself committed to the spread of more open and responsible government in the region. As Abdullah Gül confirmed in March 2006, on this point American strategy 'complies with the vision of Turkey'.[42] Turkey was admittedly reluctant to be promoted by Washington as a model, given that the project was bound to be suspect in the eyes of other Middle Eastern nations so long as at had a 'Made in the USA' label attached to it. However, as the Brussels-based International Crisis Group pointed out in June 2004, 'the message – the need for more democracy – should not be disregarded because the messenger, especially in the post-Iraq War world, is suspect'.[43] By early 2006, a more salient cause of criticism was doubt about whether the Bush administration would be consistently committed to it, given its failures in Iraq and the victory of the Islamist militants of Hamas in the Palestinian elections. Within the Republican party the appeals of palaeo- (as opposed to neo-) conservatives like Pat Buchanan seemed to have more cogency. As Buchanan argued, Iraq under Saddam Hussein had not attacked America, so America should not have attacked Iraq. In his view, the call for more democracy world-wide was 'noble-sounding nonsense', while 'our security rests on US power and will, and not on whether Zimbabwe, Sudan, Syria, Cuba or even China is ruled by tyrants'.[44] By (quite rightly) promoting the idea that the Middle East needed more democratic government, Turkey might end up holding a baby which America itself had abandoned.

Undoubtedly, the Turkish–US partnership had been damaged by events in Iraq, but this may have been for the benefit of both sides, in the sense that both had a more realistic perception of its limitations. For Turkey, it was clear that its own ability to influence US policy was limited. For the US, there was the realisation that it could not take Turkish support for granted, and that there were serious limits to the scope of the alliance. This did not mean that it had ended, however. As Richard Perle, a powerful behind-the-scenes voice in Washington policy-making, concluded, America still had 'a huge interest in the continuing demonstration that a country that is predominantly Muslim can be a democratic and secular state and can enjoy good relations with the US'.[45] Similarly, on the Turkish side, Özdem Sanberk, a former Under-Secretary at the Foreign Ministry in Ankara, urged that Turkey and America both need 'a strong bilateral relationship, one based on respect and understanding, and a willingness to let bygones be bygones, and then try to work – given the constraints of the Middle East – towards a multilateral partnership' embracing the EU and the main Middle Eastern countries.[46] What remained to be seen was whether the two sides could give concrete shape to this vision.

Notes

1. Kemal Kirişçi, 'Between Europe and the Middle East: The Transformation of Turkish Policy', *MERIA Journal*, vol. 8, no. 1, 2004, p. 1.
2. In Gül's words 'had the bill passed, we would have been taking on a job in the most ill-omened part of Iraq, and as a result maybe we would have suffered greater losses than the Americans': quoted, *Hürriyet*, 18 Apr. 2005. For Erdoğan's later remarks, see ibid., 7 Sep. 2006.
3. Ibid., 5 Feb. 2003.
4. Nasuh Uslu, Metin Toprak and İbrahim Dalmış, 'Turkish Public Opinion towards the United States in the Context of the Iraq Question', *MERIA Journal*, vol. 9, no. 3, 2005, p. 3 and Tables 5 and 14 (poll conducted in March 2003).
5. For the opposite argument, see Michael Rubin, 'Shifting Sides? The Problems of Neo-Ottomanism', *National Review Online*, 10 Aug. 2004, p. 2 (from <www.meforum.org/article/628>). Rubin proposes that the Turkish parliament's rejection of the US invasion plan 'appears more a symptom than a cause of the downturn in relations'.
6. Michael Rubin, 'Green Money, Islamist Politics in Turkey', *Middle East Quarterly*, vol. 22, no. 1, 2005, p. 5. For a highly critical response to Rubin's article, see İsmet Berkan, 'Neo-Conlar ve AKP Hükümeti', *Radikal*, 25 Feb. 2005, and 'Başbakan mesajı aldı ama ...', ibid., 26 Feb. 2005. For more of the same kind of unsupported conspiracy theories, see Frank J. Gaffney, Jr, 'Islamofascist coup?' *Washington Times*, 14 Mar. 2006.
7. Daniel Pipes, in a round-table discussion chaired by James Glazov, 'Turkey: the Road to Sharia?', *FrontPageMagazine.com*, 6 May 2005 <www.frontpagemagazine.com>, pp. 2–3. After a visit to Turkey in June 2005, Pipes admitted he had received 'quite an earful' from Turkish politicians, journalists, intellectuals and business leaders who knew his views, and that he left 'less certain of Mr Erdoğan's intentions than when I arrived', but he did not explicitly withdraw his previous claims: Daniel Pipes, 'Is Turkey Going Islamist?', *New York Sun*, 7 June 2005.
8. Graham E. Fuller, 'Don't Write off the Turks: Ankara isn't anti-American, it's Independent', *Los Angeles Times*, 11 Apr. 2005.
9. Cengiz Çandar, 'Turkish Foreign Policy and the War on Iraq', in Lenore G. Martin and Dimitris Keridis, eds, *The Future of Turkish Foreign Policy*, Cambridge MA and London: MIT Press, 2004, pp. 47 and 54. The quotation is from ibid., p. 56.
10. Philip Robins, 'Confusion at Home, Confusion Abroad: Turkey between Copenhagen and Iraq', *International Affairs*, vol. 79, no. 3, 2003, pp. 547–8 and 566. A similar criticism is made by Michael Rubin, 'A Comedy of Errors: American–Turkish Diplomacy and the Iraq War', *Turkish Policy Quarterly*, vol. 4, no. 1, 2005, p. 2.

11. Robins, 'Confusion at Home', pp. 563–4.

12. Murat Yetkin, *Tezkere: Irak Krizinin Gerçek Öyküsü*, Istanbul, Remzi, 2004, p. 276.

13. Nigar Göksel, 'Turkey and Democratization in the Middle East: A TPQ exclusive interview with Süleyman Demirel', *Turkish Policy Quarterly*, vol. 4, no. 2, 2005, p. 6.

14. Bill Park, *Turkey's Policy towards Northern Iraq: Problems and Perspectives*, London: Routledge, for International Institute for Strategic Studies, Adelphi Paper 374, 2005, p. 24.

15. See, for instance, the cartoon by Danziger, *Chicago Tribune*, 21 Feb. 2003, depicting 'our friend Turkey' as two greedy bazaar merchants walking away from an angry Uncle Sam with sacks full of dollars: there were many other examples. See also Fikret Bila, *Sivil Darbe Girişimi ve Ankara'da Irak Savaşları*, Ankara, Ümit Yayıncılık, 2003, p. 221.

16. Yetkin, *Tezkere*, p. 131.

17. *Hürriyet*, 18 May 2005 (interview with Vecdi Gönül).

18. *The Economist*, 27 Feb. 2002.

19. Robins, 'Confusion at Home', p. 560.

20. Statement by Richard Perle, in Nigar Göksel, 'Pitfalls and Opportunities for the US–Turkish Alliance: A TPQ Exclusive Interview with Richard Perle', *Turkish Policy Quarterly*, vol. 4, no. 1, 2005, p. 1.

21. As Philip Robins suggests, this probably derived from Turkey's role in the earlier Gulf crisis of 1990–1. In his words, 'a relatively small number of highly influential serving and former officials and commentators have exercised a disproportionate influence on Turkey's behalf on the inside of policy making in Washington': he includes Perle and Wolfowitz in this group. Philip Robins, *Suits and Uniforms: Turkish Foreign Policy since the Cold War*, London: Hurst, 2003, p. 18.

22. Rubin, 'Comedy of Errors', p. 2.

23. Ibid., p. 5.

24. Hasan Celal Güzel, 'Batı'nın "Kürdistan" kapanı ve Türkiye', *Radikal*, 1 Dec. 2005.

25. *Hürriyet*, 26 Feb. 2003.

26. Data from *Country Report, January 2006: Turkey*, London: Economist Intelligence Unit, 2006, p. 5.

27. Simon Jenkins, 'Sorry Sir Christopher, he wasn't even in with a shout', *The Guardian*, 9 Nov. 2005. Jenkins's comments arose from the memoirs of Sir Christopher Meyer, former British ambassador in Washington, in which Meyer argues that if Tony Blair had tried to he could have secured the postponement of the war against Iraq to the autumn of 2003: Christopher Meyer, *DC Confidential*, London: Weidenfeld & Nicolson, 2005, pp. 250 and 280–2.

28. See, e.g., Çandar, 'Turkish Foreign Policy', p. 49.

29. Yetkin, *Tezkere*, pp. 116–17.
30. Ibid., p. 276.
31. Liam Anderson and Gareth Stansfield, *The Future of Iraq: Dictatorship, Democracy or Division?*, Basingstoke and New York: Palgrave Macmillan, 2004, pp. 213–16.
32. Toby Dodge, *Iraq's Future; the Aftermath of Regime Change*, London: International Institute of Strategic Studies, Adelphi Papers No. 372, 2005, pp. 44–7.
33. *Hürriyet*, 1 Mar. 2006.
34. Website of NTV television, Istanbul <www.ntvmsnbc.com> 18 Nov. 2005.
35. Website of CNN-Turk television, Istanbul <www.cnnturk.com> 19 Nov. 2005.
36. Mehmet Ali Birand, 'Bush's Warning to Barzani', *Turkish Daily News*, 27 Oct. 2005, and 'A Nice Development for Cyprus', ibid., 28 Oct. 2005 (originally published in *Son Posta*, same dates).
37. Ibid., 1 Mar. 2006.
38. Ziya Öniş and Suhnaz Yılmaz, 'The Turkey–EU–US Triangle in Perspective: Transformation or Continuity?', *Middle East Journal*, vol. 59, no. 2, 2005, p. 266. The same point is made by Mark Parris, 'Allergic Partners: Can US–Turkish Relations be Saved?', *Turkish Policy Quarterly*, vol.4, no. 1, 2005, p. 3.
39. Ian O. Lesser, 'Off Autopilot: The Future of Turkish–US Relations', ibid., vol. 4, no. 4, 2005, p. 3.
40. In France, the picture was complicated by the fact that, while President Chirac was prepared to support Turkish accession to the EU, Nicolas Sarkozy, the leader of his own party, opposed it – making the definition of a 'European' policy still more difficult.
41. Ian O. Lesser, 'Turkey and the United States: Anatomy of a Strategic Relationship', in Martin and Keridis, eds, *Future of Turkish Foreign Policy*, p. 85.
42. Quoted, *Turkish Daily News*, 6 Mar. 2006.
43. International Crisis Group, *Middle East and North Africa Briefing: The Broader Middle East and North Africa Initiative; Imperilled at Birth*, Brussels/Amman: International Crisis Group, 7 June 2004, p. 1.
44. Quoted, *The Economist*, 11 Feb. 2006.
45. Richard Perle, in Göksel , 'Pitfalls and Opportunities', p. 6.
46. Özdem Sanberk, 'Turkey and the US: A Renewed Alliance?' *Turkish Daily News*, 6 June 2005.

Bibliography

OFFICIAL DOCUMENTS

Turkey: Başbakanlık İnsan Hakları Danışma Kurulu, '*Azınlık Hakları ve Kültürel Haklar Çalışma Grubu' Raporu, Ekim 2004* (Ankara, Prime Minister's Office, Human Rights Advisory Board, 2004).

Iraq: Transitional Administrative Law of 4 March 2004: text from <www.fco.gov.uk/files/kfile/TAL>.

Iraq: Draft constitution of 2005: from the website of the Iraqi Transitional Government <www.iraqigovernment.org>.

SERIAL PUBLICATIONS

Country Report, Turkey (London, Economist Intelligence Unit, quarterly).

Country Profile, Turkey (London, Economist Intelligence Unit, annual).

Statistical Yearbook of Turkey (Ankara, State Institute of Statistics, annual).

TURKISH NEWS MEDIA

Briefing (Ankara, weekly).

Hürriyet (Istanbul, daily <www.hurriyet.com.tr>).

Milliyet (Istanbul, daily <www.milliyet.com.tr>).

Radikal (Istanbul, daily <www.radikal.com.tr>).

Turkish Daily News (Ankara, daily <www.turkishdailynews.com.tr>).

Website of CNN-Türk television, Istanbul <www.cnnturk.com>.

Website of NTV television, Istanbul <www.ntvmsnbc.com>.

Zaman (Istanbul, daily <www.zaman.com.tr>).

BOOKS AND ARTICLES
(Excludes signed newspaper articles)

Akşin, Aptülhat, *Atatürk'ün Dış Politika İlkeleri ve Diplomasisi*, Ankara: Türk Tarih Kurumu, 1991.

Albayrak, Mustafa, *Türk Siyasi Tarihinde Demokrat Parti*, Ankara: Phoenix, 2004.

Aliriza, Bülent, 'Turkey and the Global Storm', *Insight Turkey* (Istanbul, quarterly), vol. 3, no. 4, 2001.

Al-Marashi, Ibrahim, 'Iraq's Constitutional Debate', *MERIA Journal*, vol. 9, no. 3, 2005.

Anderson, Liam, and Gareth Stansfield, *The Future of Iraq: Dictatorship, Democracy or Division?*, Basingstoke and New York: Palgrave Macmillan, 2004.

Aral, Berdal, 'Dispensing with Tradition? Turkish Politics and International Society during the Özal Decade', *Middle Eastern Studies*, vol. 37, no. 1, 2001.

Atacan, Fulya, 'Explaining Religious Politics at the Crossroad: AKP-SP', *Turkish Studies*, vol. 6, no. 2, 2005.

Ataman, Mühittin, 'Özal Leadership and the Restructuring of Turkish Ethnic Policy in the 1980s', *Middle Eastern Studies*, vol. 38, no. 4, 2002.

Athanassopoulou, Ekavi, *Turkey–Anglo-American Security Interests, 1945–1952: the First Enlargement of NATO*, London: Cass, 1999.

Aykan, Mahmut Balı, 'The Turkey–US–Israel Triangle: Continuity, Change and Implications for Turkey's Post-Cold War Middle East Policy', *Journal of South Asian and Middle Eastern Studies*, vol. 22, no. 4, 1999.

—— 'Turkey's Perspectives on Turkish–US Relations concerning Persian Gulf Security in the Post-Cold War Era, 1989–1995', *Middle East Journal*, vol. 50, no. 3, 1996.

—— 'Turkey's Policy in Northern Iraq, 1991–95', *Middle Eastern Studies*, vol. 32, no. 4, 1996.

Barkey, Henri J., 'The Silent Victor: Turkey's Role in the Gulf War', in Efraim Karsh, ed., *The Iran–Iraq War: Impact and Implications*, London: Macmillan, in association with Jafee Center for Strategic Studies, Tel Aviv University, 1989.

—— and Graham E. Fuller, 'Turkey's Kurdish Question: Critical Turning Points and Missed Opportunities', *Middle East Journal*, vol. 51, no. 1, 1997.

Beck, Peter J., '"A Tedious and Perilous Controversy": Britain and the

Settlement of the Mosul Dispute', *Middle Eastern Studies*, vol. 17, no. 2, 1981.

Bengio, Ofra, *The Turkish–Israeli Relationship: Changing Ties of Middle Eastern Outsiders*, New York NY and Basingstoke, Palgrave Macmillan, 2004.

Bila, Fikret, *Sivil Darbe Girişimı ve Ankara'da Irak Savaşları*, Ankara: Ümit Yayıncılık, 2003.

Bilge, A. Suat, et al., *Olaylarla Türk Dış Politikası (1919–1965)*, Ankara University: Political Science Faculty, 1969.

Birand, Mehmet Ali, and Soner Yalçın, eds, *The Özal: Bir Davanın Öyküsü*, Istanbul: Doğan, 2001.

Blackwell, Stephen, 'A Desert Squall: Anglo-American Planning for Military Intervention in Iraq, July 1958–August 1959', *Middle Eastern Studies*, vol. 35, no. 3, 1999.

Bölükbaşı, Suha, 'Turkey Challenges Iraq and Syria: the Euphrates Dispute', *Journal of South Asian and Middle Eastern Studies*, vol. 16, no. 4, 1993.

Bush, George W., 'President's Remarks at Galatasaray University', 29 June 2004: from the White House website <www.whitehouse.gov/news/releases/2004/06>.

Çağaptay, Soner, 'Where Goes the US–Turkish Relationship?', *Middle East Quarterly*, vol. 11, no. 4, 2004.

Çakır, Ruşen, and Fehmi Çalmuk, *Recep Tayyip Erdoğan: Bir Dönüşüm Öyküsü*, Istanbul: Metis, 2001.

Campany, Richard C., Jr., *Turkey and the United States: the Arms Embargo Period*, New York: Praeger, 1986.

Campbell, John C., *Defense of the Middle East: Problems of American Policy*, New York: Praeger, 1960.

Çandar, Cengiz, 'Turkish Foreign Policy and the War on Iraq', in Lenore G. Martin and Dimitris Keridis, eds, *The Future of Turkish Foreign Policy*, Cambridge MA and London: MIT Press, 2004.

Cemal, Hasan, *Özal Hikayesi*, Ankara and Istanbul: Bilgi, 1989.

Çetin, Bilal, *Türk Siyasetinde bir Kasımpaşalı: Tayyip Erdoğan*, Istanbul, Gündem: 2003.

Coşar, Nevin, and Sevtap Demirci, 'The Mosul Question and the Turkish Republic: Before and After the Frontier Treaty, 1926', *Middle Eastern Studies*, vol. 42, no. 1, 2006.

Council on Foreign Relations, Washington DC, 'National Defense in the Second Term', Council on Foreign Relations, Washington DC, 17 February 2005: from the Council's website <www.cfr.org/

publication/7858/national>.

Dalacoura, Katerina, 'US Democracy Promotion in the Middle East since 11 September 2001: A Critique', *International Affairs*, vol. 81, no. 5, 2005.

Demirel, Süleyman, *see* Göksel, Nigar.

Deringil, Selim, *Turkish Foreign Policy during the Second World War: an 'Active' Neutrality*, Cambridge: Cambridge University Press, 1989.

Dodge, Toby, *Iraq's Future; the Aftermath of Regime Change*, London: International Institute of Strategic Studies, Adelphi Papers no. 372, 2005.

Evans, Stephen F., *The Slow Rapprochement: Britain and Turkey in the Age of Kemal Ataturk*, Walkington: Eothen Press, 1982.

Finkel, Caroline, *Osman's Dream: the Story of the Ottoman Empire, 1300–1923*, London: John Murray, 2005.

Firat, Melek, and Ömer Kürkçüoğlu, 'Arap Devletleriyle İlişkiler', in Baskın Oran, ed., *Türk Dış Politikası: Kurtuluş Savaşından Bügüne: Olgular, Belgeler, Yorumlar*, Istanbul: İletişim, 2001.

Glazov, James, ed., 'Turkey: the Road to Sharia?', *FrontPageMagazine.com*, 6 May 2005 <www.frontpagemagazine.com>.

Göksel, Nigar, 'Pitfalls and Opportunities for the US–Turkish Alliance: A TPQ Exclusive Interview with Richard Perle', *Turkish Policy Quarterly*, vol. 4, no. 1, 2005.

—— 'Turkey and Democratization in the Middle East: A TPQ exclusive interview with Süleyman Demirel', *Turkish Policy Quarterly*, vol. 4, no. 2, 2005.

Görener, Aylin Şeker, 'US Policy Towards Iraq: Moral Dilemmas of Sanctions and Regime Change', *Turkish Review of Middle East Studies* (Istanbul: annual) vol. 12, 2001.

Gözen, Ramazan, 'Küzey Irak Sorunu', in İdris Bal, ed., *21 Yüzyılın Eşiğinde Türk Dış Politikası*, Istanbul: Alfa, 2001.

—— 'Türkiye'nin II Körfez Savaşı Politikası: Aktif Politika ve Sonuçları', in İdris Bal, ed., *21 Yüzyılın Eşiğinde Türk Dış Politikası*, Istanbul: Alfa, 2001.

Grigoriadis, Ioannis, *Turkish Political Culture and the European Union*, Ph.D. thesis, School of Oriental and African Studies, University of London, 2005.

Gündoğdu, Ayten, 'Identities in Question: Greek–Turkish Relations in a Period of Transformation' *MERIA Journal*, vol. 5, no. 1, 2000.

Güney, Aylin, 'The People's Democracy Party', in Barry Rubin and Metin Heper, eds, *Political Parties in Turkey*, London: Cass, 2002.

Gunter, Michael M., 'The Foreign Policy of the Iraqi Kurds', *Journal of South Asian and Middle Eastern Studies*, vol. 20, no. 3, 1997.
—— *The Kurds and the Future of Turkey*, New York: St Martin's Press, 1997.
—— *The Kurds in Turkey*, Boulder CO: Westview, 1990.
—— 'The Silent Coup: The Secularist–Islamist Struggle in Turkey', *Journal of South Asian and Middle Eastern Studies*, vol. 21, no. 3, 1998.
Gürkan, İhsan, 'Turkish–Iraqi Relations: the Cold War and its Aftermath', *Turkish Review of Middle East Studies* (Istanbul: annual) vol. 9, 1996–7.
Hale, William, *Turkish Foreign Policy, 1774–2000*, 2nd edn, London and Portland OR: Frank Cass, 2002.
Harris, George S., *Troubled Alliance: Turkish–American Problems in Historical Perpective, 1945–1971*, Washington DC: American Enterprise Institute for Public Policy Research and Hoover Institution, 1972.
Henze, Paul B., 'Turkey: Toward the Twenty-First Century', in Graham E. Fuller and Ian O. Lesser, eds, *Turkey's New Geopolitics: From the Balkans to Western China*, Boulder, CO: Westview, 1993.
Heper, Metin, and Şule Toktaş, 'Islam, Modernity and Democracy in Contemporary Turkey: The Case of Recep Tayyip Erdoğan', *Muslim World*, vol. 95, no. 2, 2003.
Hersh, Seymour M., *Chain of Command*, London: Penguin, 2005.
Hirszowicz, Lukasz, *The Third Reich and the Arab East*, London: Routledge & Kegan Paul, 1966.
Hurewitz, J. C., ed., *Diplomacy in the Near and Middle East: A Diplomatic Record, 1914–1956*, Princeton NJ: Van Nostrand, 1956.
İlhan, Üzgel, 'ABD ve NATO'yla İlişkiler', in Baskın Oran, ed., *Türk Dış Politikası: Kurtuluş Savaşından Bügüne: Olgular, Belgeler, Yorumlar*, Istanbul: İletişim, 2001.
İlkin, Selim, 'The Chester Railway Project', in Türkiye İş Bankası, *International Symposium on Ataturk (17–22 May 1981)*, Ankara: Türkiye İş Bankası Kültür Yayınları, 1984.
International Crisis Group, *Iraq: Allaying Turkey's Fears over Kurdish Ambitions*, Brussels: International Crisis Group, Middle East Report no. 35, 26 January 2005.
—— *Middle East and North Africa Briefing: The Broader Middle East and North Africa Initiative; Imperilled at Birth*, Brussels/Amman: International Crisis Group, 7 June 2004.
Jung, Dietrich, 'The Sèvres Syndrome: Turkish Foreign Policy and its Historical Legacies', *American Diplomacy*, vol. 8, no. 2, 2003.
Karpat, Kemal H., 'Turkish and Arab–Israeli Relations', in Kemal H. Karpat

et al., *Turkey's Foreign Policy in Transition*, Leiden: Brill, 1975.

Kirişçi, Kemal, 'Between Europe and the Middle East: the Transformation of Turkish Policy', *MERIA Journal*, vol. 8, no. 4, 2004.

—— 'Provide Comfort or Trouble: Operation Provide Comfort and its Impact on Turkish Foreign Policy', *Turkish Review of Middle East Studies*, Istanbul: Ortadoğu ve Balkan İncelemeleri Vakfı (annual) vol. 8, 1994/5.

—— 'The Kurdish Question and Turkish Foreign Policy', in Lenore G. Martin and Dimitris Keridis, eds, *The Future of Turkish Foreign Policy*, Cambridge MA and London: MIT Press, 2004.

—— 'Turkey and the Kurdish Safe Haven in Northern Iraq', *Journal of South Asian and Middle Eastern Studies*, vol. 19, no. 3, 1995.

—— and Gareth Winrow, *The Kurdish Question and Turkey: an Example of Trans-state Ethnic Conflict*, London: Cass, 1997.

Kubicek, Paul, 'The Earthquake, Europe, and Prospects for Political Change in Turkey', *MERIA Journal*, vol. 5, no. 2, 2000.

Lesser, Ian O., 'Off Autopilot: the Future of Turkish–US Relations', *Turkish Policy Quarterly*, vol. 4, no. 4, 2005.

—— 'Turkey and the United States: Anatomy of a Strategic Relationship', in Lenore G. Martin and Dimitris Keridis, eds, *The Future of Turkish Foreign Policy*, Cambridge MA, and London: MIT Press, 2004.

McDowall, David, *A Modern History of the Kurds*, London: I. B. Tauris, 1996.

McGhee, George C., *The US–Turkish–NATO Middle East Connection*, London: Macmillan, 1990.

Mango, Andrew, 'Ataturk and the Kurds', *Middle Eastern Studies*, vol. 35, no. 4, 1999.

Martin, Lenore G., 'Turkey's Middle East Foreign Policy', in Lenore G. Martin and Dimitris Keridis, eds, *The Future of Turkish Foreign Policy*, Cambridge MA and London: MIT Press, 2004.

Meyer, Christopher, *DC Confidential*, London: Weidenfeld & Nicolson, 2005.

Olmert, Y., 'Britain, Turkey and the Levant Question during the Second World War', *Middle Eastern Studies*, vol. 23, no. 4, 1987.

Olson, Robert, 'The Kurdish Question and Turkey's Foreign Policy, 1991– 1995: From the Gulf War to the Incursion into Iraq', *Journal of South Asian and Middle Eastern Studies*, vol. 19, no. 1, 1995.

Öniş, Ziya, and Şuhnaz Yılmaz, 'The Turkey–EU–US Triangle in Perspective: Transformation or Continuity?', *Middle East Journal*, vol. 59, no. 2, 2005.

Oran, Baskın, *Türkiye'de Azınlıklar, Kavramlar, Lozan, İç Mevzuat, İçtihat, Uygulama*, Istanbul: Turkish Economic and Social Studies Foundation [TESEV] 2004.

Özal, Turgut, 'President Turgut Özal's Address to the Global Panel sponsored by the European Studies Centre in Amsterdam', and 'President Özal's TV Speech concerning Turkish Help to Iraqi Refugees' (31 May 1991), in *Studies on Turkish–Arab Relations: Special Issue on the Gulf Crisis*, Istanbul: Foundation for Studies on Turkish–Arab Relations, annual, vol. 6, 1991.

Özbudun, Ergun, and Serap Yazıcı, *Democratization Reforms in Turkey (1993–2004)*, Istanbul: Turkish Economic and Social Studies Foundation [TESEV] 2004.

Paker, Hamde, 'Particularistic Interactions: State (In)Capacity, Civil Society, and Disaster Management', in Fikret Adaman and Murat Arsel, eds, *Environmentalism in Turkey: Between Democracy and Development?*, Aldershot and Burlington VT: Ashgate, 2005.

Park, Bill, 'Between Europe, the United States and the Middle East: Turkey and European Security in the Wake of the Iraq Crisis', *Perspectives on European Politics and Society*, vol. 5, no. 3, Leiden: Brill, 2004.

—— 'Iraq's Kurds and Turkey: Challenges for US Policy', *Parameters*, vol. 34, no. 3, 2004.

—— 'Turkey, the United States and Northern Iraq', in Paul Cornish, ed., *The Conflict in Iraq, 2003*, Basingstoke and New York: Palgrave Macmillan, 2004.

—— *Turkey's Policy towards Northern Iraq: Problems and Perspectives*, London: International Institute for Strategic Studies, Adelphi Paper 374, 2005.

Parris, Mark, 'Allergic Partners: Can US–Turkish Relations be Saved?', *Turkish Policy Quarterly*, vol. 4, no. 1, 2005.

—— 'Turkey and the US: A Partnership Rediscovered', *Insight Turkey*, vol. 3 no. 4, 2001.

Perincek, Doğu, ed., *Mustafa Kemal Eskişehir İzmit Konuşmaları*, Istanbul: Kaynak, 1993.

Perle, Richard, *see* Göksel, Nigar.

Pope, Hugh, 'Digging into Iraq', *Middle East International*, 27 November 1992.

Pope, Nicole and Hugh Pope, *Turkey Unveiled: Ataturk and After*, London: John Murray, 1997.

Ritter, Scott, *Iraq Confidential: The Untold Story of America's Intelligence*

Conspiracy, London: I. B. Tauris, 2005.

Robins, Philip, 'Confusion at Home, Confusion Abroad: Turkey between Copenhagen and Iraq', *International Affairs*, vol. 79, no. 3, 2003.

—— 'Turkish Foreign Policy under Erbakan', *Survival*, vol. 39, Summer 1997.

—— *Suits and Uniforms: Turkish Foreign Policy Since the Cold War*, London: Hurst, 2003.

—— *Turkey and the Middle East*, London: Pinter, for Royal Institute of International Affairs, 1991.

Robinson, Richard D., *The First Turkish Republic*, Cambridge MA: Harvard University Press, 1963.

Rubin, Michael, 'A Comedy of Errors: American-Turkish Diplomacy and the Iraq War', *Turkish Policy Quarterly*, vol. 4, no. 1, 2005.

—— 'Green Money, Islamist Politics in Turkey', *Middle East Quarterly*, vol. 22, no. 1, 2005.

—— 'Shifting Sides? The Problems of Neo-Ottomanism', *National Review Online*, 10 August 2004 (from <www.meforum.org/article/628>).

—— 'The Future of Iraq: Democracy, Civil War or Chaos?', *MERIA Journal*, vol. 9, no. 3, 2005.

Sakallıoğlu, Ümıt Cizre, 'Historicisizing the Present and Problematizing the Future of the Kurdish Problem: A Critique of the TOBB Report on the Eastern Question', *New Perspectives on Turkey*, no. 14, 1996.

Sanjian, Ara, 'The Formulation of the Baghdad Pact', *Middle Eastern Studies*, vol. 33, no. 2, 1997.

Sever, Ayşegül, 'The Compliant Ally? Turkey and the West in the Middle East, 1954–58', *Middle Eastern Studies*, vol. 34, no. 2, 1998.

Torumtay, Necip, *Orgeneral Torumtay'ın Anıları*, Istanbul: Milliyet, 1994.

Tripp, Charles, *A History of Iraq*, Cambridge: Cambridge University Press, 2000.

Turan, Ali Eşref, *Türkıye'de Seçmen Davranışı: Öncekceki Kırılmalar ve 2002 Seçimi*, Istanbul: Bilgi Ünıversitesi Yayınları, 2004.

Uslu, Nasuh, Metin Toprak, İbrahim Dalmış and Ertan Aydın, 'Turkish Public Opinion towards the United States in the Context of the Iraq Question', *MERIA Journal*, vol. 9, no. 3, 2005.

Vali, Ferenc A., *Bridge Across the Bosporus: The Foreign Policy of Turkey*, Baltimore MD and London: Johns Hopkins University Press, 1971.

Weber, Frank G., *The Evasive Neutral: Germany, Britain and the Quest for a Turkish Alliance in the Second World War*, Columbia MO and London: University of Missouri Press, 1979.

Yavuz, M. Hakan, *Islamic Political Identity in Turkey*, Oxford: Oxford University Press, 2003.

—— and Nihat Ali Özcan, 'The Kurdish Question and Turkey's Justice and Development Party', *Middle East Policy*, vol. 13, no. 1, 2006.

Yazıcıoğlu, M. Sait, 'Özal'in İslam Anlayışı ve Dini Özgürlükler', in İhsan Sezal and İhsan Dağı, eds, *Özal: Siyaset, İktisat, Zihniyet*, Istanbul: Boyut, 2001.

Yetkin, Murat, *Tezkere: Irak Krizinin Gerçek Öyküsü*, Istanbul: Remzi, 2004.

Index

Personal names: Arabs are indexed under their first names, with cross-references where necessary; all others are indexed under their family names

About the London Middle East Institute

The London Middle East Institute (LMEI) of SOAS is a charitable, tax-exempt organisation whose purpose is to promote knowledge of all aspects of the Middle East, both among the general public and to those with special interests in the region. Drawing on the expertise of over seventy SOAS academic Middle East specialists, accessing the substantial library and other resources of SOAS, and interacting with over 300 individual and corporate affiliates, the LMEI since its founding in 2002 has sponsored conferences, seminars and exhibitions; conducted training programmes; and undertaken consultancies for public and private sector clients. The LMEI publishes a monthly magazine – The Middle East in London – and with Saqi it publishes four books annually in the SOAS Middle East Issues series. These activities are guided by a Board of Trustees on which is represented SOAS, the British Academy, the University of London, the Foreign and Commonwealth Office and private sector interests.

Professor Robert Springborg

MBI Chair in Middle East Studies
Director, London Middle East Institute
School of Oriental and African Studies
Russell Square, London WC1H 0XG
United Kingdom

www.lmei.soas.ac.uk